Gulf Energy
and the World

GULF ENERGY
AND THE WORLD

Challenges and
Threats

THE EMIRATES CENTER FOR STRATEGIC
STUDIES AND RESEARCH

Published in 1997 by
The Emirates Center for Strategic Studies and Research
PO Box 4567, Abu Dhabi, United Arab Emirates

Copyright © 1997 by The Emirates Center for Strategic Studies
and Research

Distributed by British Academic Press
an imprint of I.B.Tauris, Victoria House
Bloomsbury Square, London WC1 4DZ
175 Fifth Avenue, New York NY10010

A full CIP record for this book is available from the British Library
A full CIP record for this book is available from the Library
of Congress

Library of Congress catalog card number: available

ISBN 1 86064 210 1 hardback
ISBN 1 86064 211 X paperback

Typeset by the Harrington Consultancy, London EC1

Contents

Abbreviations and Acronyms

/b	per barrel
bcm	billion cubic meters
b/d	barrels per day
boe	barrel of oil equivalent
BTU	British Thermal Unit
CERI	Canadian Energy Research Institute
cif	cost, insurance and freight
CIS	Commonwealth of Independent States
DoE	Department of Energy
E/D	Exploration and development
EE	East European
EU	European Union
EV	electric vehicle
FOB	free on board
FPSO	floating production storage and off-loading vessel
FSU	former Soviet Union
GCC	Gulf Cooperation Council
GDP	gross domestic product
GNP	gross national product
IEA	International Energy Agency
IEE	Institute of Energy Economics, Japan
IEW	International Energy Workshop
LNG	liquefied natural gas
LPG	liquefied petroleum gas
Mcf	thousand cubic feet
MTOE	million tonnes oil equivalent
NGL	natural gas liquids
NOC	national oil company
NOPEC	non-OPEC
OAPEC	Organization of Arab Petroleum Exporting Countries
OECD	Organization for Economic Cooperation and Development
OPEC	Organization of Petroleum Exporting Countries
ROK	Republic of Korea
RP	reserve per production
TCF	trillion cubic feet
TOE	tonnes oil equivalent
UAE	United Arab Emirates
WTI	West Texas Intermediate

Note: Not all acronyms used in this book are listed above.

Foreword

The challenges facing Gulf countries today can be better understood with the introduction of fresh ideas and adaptation of new approaches to domestic and regional issues. What is needed is a new strategy that will optimize and make use of available alternatives most effectively. As scholars and analysts, it is the mission of the Emirates Center for Strategic Studies and Research (ECSSR) to contribute to the understanding of the current processes that ultimately affect the very basis of our society. It is our duty to strengthen our knowledge of the current events that have a direct impact on Gulf energy. The information enclosed in this book attempts to provide an accurate and objective picture of the present situation and future challenges. These challenges can and must be met straight on as Gulf economies race towards the 21st century.

This book is a collection of ECSSR attempts to evaluate the current and future trends in the world energy markets. A variety of topics discussed in the book provide a better understanding of the future of the Gulf and its contribution to these markets. An objective analytical review of the forces that influence Gulf energy is offered. In addition, other pertinent issues that affect the Gulf region as a global supplier of energy resources are addressed.

The position of the Gulf region in the world energy arena is no longer as secure and stable as it was two decades ago. The region has experienced a number of provocations in the past fifteen years. Oil production from non-OPEC countries is competing aggressively with OPEC oil. Conservation and environmental concerns in oil-importing countries tend to dominate the political agenda of these countries. Furthermore, technological breakthroughs are lowering the cost of alternative energy. Meanwhile, domestic budgetary constraints are diverting funds into social welfare programs instead of new production technologies. These financial demands are likely to grow. Moreover, with a world economy that continues to remain somewhat stagnant, political instability cannot be ruled out.

Nevertheless, the growing energy demand in a number of Asian economies is opening up windows of opportunity for Gulf oil and gas producers. In addition, the welfare benefits from freer trade among countries is expected to further increase the demand for oil and gas.

Jamal S. Al-Suwaidi, Ph.D., Director
The Emirates Center for Strategic Studies and Research

Introduction

The Gulf Cooperation Council (GCC) bloc plays a leading role in the world energy market. Its members – Bahrain, Kuwait, Oman, Qatar, Saudi Arabia, and the United Arab Emirates (UAE) hold nearly 46 percent of the world's crude oil reserves and 14 percent of global natural gas reserves. In 1994, these countries accounted for approximately 46.7 percent of the world oil trade.

The GCC states are highly dependent on revenues from the export of crude oil and natural gas, although revenues from gas are still relatively modest. These countries, while rich in oil and gas reserves, have limited non-hydrocarbon-related resources or industry. Despite economic diversification efforts to increase non-oil contributions to the gross domestic product (GDP), Council members still rely primarily on the oil sector to drive their national economies.

Oil production policies in the GCC grouping have been influenced by the Organization of Petroleum Exporting Countries (OPEC), of which Kuwait, Qatar, Saudi Arabia, and the UAE are members. This has not always served the best interests of the Council members. Saudi Arabia, in particular, suffered from its role as the so-called swing producer of OPEC in the 1980s. Because not all GCC members are members of OPEC, there have always been some differences in rationalizing the national oil output policies of the Gulf producers.

Between 1980 and 1994, total world demand for crude oil rose from around 61 million barrels per day to nearly 67 million barrels, at an average annual rate of about 0.7 percent. GCC countries, as a whole, did not exploit this increase in demand. In fact, compared to the 1980 level, their overall daily average declined slightly.

The reasons for the decline in the GCC's share of the world oil market are many. It is clear that increases in oil output from non-OPEC, non-GCC sources are making an impact. One count identifies some 62 non-OPEC producers in 1994. Though few of these are sources of massive exports, as a whole, they do compete with the output from OPEC and the Council.

The erosion in the Gulf Cooperation Council's share in the world oil market has been marked. Beginning in the early 1980s and accelerating towards the middle of that decade, the decline in oil revenues resulting from both lower exports and lower prices threatened the positive growth rates of several

I

GCC economies. Saudi Arabia bore the brunt as it had to slash its production from a high of nearly 10.25 million barrels per day in 1981 to a low of 3.43 million barrels per day in 1985. Heavy spending on infrastructure and human resource development was exacerbated by the costs of the 1990–91 Gulf conflict, which moved some GCC members from capital-surplus to capital-deficit status and necessitated borrowing to finance their national budgets.

The year 1986 was a turning point for GCC producers. While total world demand for crude oil increased at an annual average rate of only 1.24 percent between 1985 and 1994, production in the GCC states rose at a much faster rate of approximately 8.87 percent per annum. The general effect has been to recapture a portion of the market lost during the earlier years.

What factors contributed to this increase in GCC production? And will these factors continue to prevail in the future? In all likelihood, the GCC states will have to face the challenge of maintaining and, if possible, increasing market share in global oil trade.

Aside from meeting increasing domestic consumption and demand for the downstream activities in refining and petrochemicals, the United Nations embargo on Iraqi exports has helped in keeping worldwide supply and demand well balanced. Furthermore, the United States continues as well to boycott oil from both Iran and Libya and is pressuring other countries to follow suit. This boycott will not last indefinitely, although Iranian output may be nearing its installed production capacity at this time. The free movement of output from the countries now politically constrained could have an influence on the economies of the GCC states only if the supply–demand balance is seriously jeopardized over a prolonged period.

The breakup of the Soviet Union resulted in a declining crude oil output that has given the GCC states an opportunity to capture a portion of the markets traditionally supplied by the former Soviet Union (FSU) states. The independent countries of Kazakhstan, Azerbaijan, Turkmenistan, and other FSU states are viewed as potentially the largest new sources of supply. Russia and the successor countries view the oil sector as a critical foreign-exchange earner and an economic activity that can attract substantial foreign investment. Whether the FSU becomes a serious challenger for the GCC market share depends on the time frame within which pipelines and transit routes can be agreed upon and implemented as well as on the achievement of a level of political and regulatory stability for joint-venture partners.

The lower worldwide finding costs for replacement of reserves impacts indirectly on the pricing of crude oil because of the availability of supplies. However, few areas can match the GCC for the size of reserves, low extraction costs, and thus the return on investment. Nonetheless, the GCC producers remain extremely sensitive to the level of oil-generated revenue because of the heavy reliance on the petroleum sector to finance government expenditure.

The issue of the GCC's market share of oil trade reflects two primary concerns. First is the aspect of competition engendered by supply realities. Despite an increase in non-OPEC output, especially since 1980, the vastness of the Gulf reserves and the limited size of new reserves additions – aside from the FSU – clearly indicate that, if world oil demand were to remain constant at its existing level and did not rise, the OPEC and GCC share will likely increase in the medium term (10 to 15 years).

The second aspect of competition for GCC crude oil is from other sources of energy, including natural gas, nuclear, coal, renewables, and non-conventional forms. For example, new electric generating plants that receive multinational aid or commercial bank financing are dual-fired, preferably with fuel-switching capabilities between fuel oil and natural gas. Increased energy efficiency in processes and equipment have served to dampen some of the rising demand for total primary energy consumption. Similarly, breakthroughs have extended the life of some of the oil reserves or made enhanced recovery economically feasible. Such unanticipated developments can impact on the supply–demand balance, particularly in the near future (5 to 10 years).

Along with the price-induced conservation approaches after 1973–74 and again in 1979–80, consumption and fuel choice go hand-in-hand with growing environmental awareness. Increased energy efficiency and regulations that favor fuels with lower carbon emissions could affect the market as well.

The "threat" confronting the GCC states is the diversity of elements that could impact on future markets. To counteract this threat, the GCC members may need to adopt long-term strategies to hold and expand existing markets and to penetrate into emerging markets. They need to assess the extent to which they can offset negative effects of international oil price fluctuations and strengthen their negotiating position in the world market.

In the quest to attain some degree of security for their exports of crude, the GCC members have undertaken several strategies, including downstream operations in major consuming/importing areas such as Europe, the Far East, and even the United States. However, the downstream linkages in foreign countries must be economically viable as the products face stiff competition. Note that oil consumption is growing fastest in the emerging economies of the South and Southeast Asian states. While crude oil use in the US rose approximately 3.6 percent in 1994 as compared to 1980 levels, use in South and Southeast Asia, Australasia, and the Pacific region nearly doubled in the same period. Consumption in both the European Union (EU) and FSU countries declined in that span.

This book is a compilation of seven papers that examine the general setting and history of the international oil market. It also analyzes the role of the Gulf countries within this arena, the current opportunities within the oil market, and the threats and challenges facing the Gulf nations. The chapters chronicle past events, investigate present market conditions, highlight new developments, and forecast events using current knowledge about the industry.

To begin with, Paul Stevens describes the economics of the oil industry, chronologically lists events that have influenced the international oil market, and introduces the Gulf oil-producing countries in the context of the international oil market. Specifically, Stevens looks at the role the Gulf countries play in shaping the structure of the industry and its impact on expectations in the global oil market.

Vahan Zanoyan expresses his discontent with the way the international oil market is analyzed. In this regard, he suggests an alternative method. He makes several useful observations, to focus on actual patterns of trade among key exporting and importing geographic regions regardless of whether oil suppliers fall into OPEC or *non-OPEC* groups or oil consumers fall into OECD or *non-OECD* groups. Furthermore, he believes that the actual supply of crude in the world market is dependent on such items as commercial factors, domestic economic dependence, international embargoes, a country's financial capabilities, expectations of crude oil demand, and the effect of speculation in the commodity market. In much the same way, Zanoyan believes that the demand for oil in consuming countries is dependent upon the existence of current and planned international refinery capacities, strategic reserves, information on new oil finds, level of economic activity, and a consuming country's capacity to store various petroleum products, among other things.

Ken Koyama looks at developments in the Asian economies. He finds that the rapid economic growth in these countries is accompanied by increases in the demand for oil. A significant portion of this oil is supplied by Gulf producers. Although Koyama expects economic growth and development to continue in most Asian countries, he observes that many of these countries are increasingly using other energy sources to satisfy their needs. He further notes that although environmental concerns provide one reason for the shift in the source of energy, it is clearly not the only reason. As Asian countries are highly dependent on foreign energy sources, they are initiating marked efforts to reduce their dependence on any one region. Leaving these concerns aside, Koyama reasons that the limited oil resources of the Asian countries will continue to increase their dependence on outside producers.

Thomas Stauffer highlights the thinking that certain Gulf countries and OPEC members are undermining their own interests by producing and exporting gas. He sees gas competing Btu by Btu against oil. As such, the opportunity cost of producing gas is income from the sale of oil.

Stauffer would not object if the net increase in income from gas sales were greater than the net decrease in the income from lower oil sales. But, as he observes, this is not the case. He indicates that because gas production and distribution requires heavy investment, overall production costs are decidedly increased. Given that declining oil prices also lower the price at which gas is sold, the lower prices leave a relatively smaller margin for the producer as compared to the margin on oil sales. As such, the producer's net income declines by selling gas rather than oil.

Michael Lynch's chapter documents various estimates and forecasts of reserves and production in the former Soviet Union countries. It compiles and classifies these forecasts from the most optimistic to the most pessimistic and shows how the forecasts are scattered. Based on these forecasts, estimates of reserves, capacity, and new investments, Lynch estimates the effect of the oil supply from the FSU countries on the international market, in both the near and distant future.

Abdul-Razak Faris Al-Faris investigates the effect of increasing domestic oil consumption on oil export revenues in the Gulf countries. He uses an econometric model to estimate and forecast gasoline consumption. He concludes that if the trend of rising domestic demand for gasoline in the Gulf countries continues to rise, eventually a more significant portion of these states' oil production will be used to meet the domestic demand. As such, unless capacity increases proportionately, the Gulf states' revenues from oil exports will decline.

Walid Khadduri contends that, in the foreseeable future, the Gulf countries will face a more difficult task selling crude in the international market. It is his observation that OPEC's role in the world oil market has become secondary. He believes this is, in part, due to increases in supply from non-OPEC countries, and also due to successful conservation efforts in the consuming nations. Furthermore, Khadduri observes that OPEC's negotiating strength has deteriorated due to the increasing dependence of the respective member countries on revenues from oil exports. This increase in dependence is attributed to economic mismanagement in the member countries.

Taken all together, this compilation of papers provides an energy trend assessment and analysis of the future relationship of oil and gas to the world economy with a primary focus on the near-term UAE and GCC energy markets choices and constraints. The authors make it clear that while the Gulf region is uniquely placed to continue to play a crucial role in the world energy markets, potential threats to this position exist. They also underline the need for the Gulf region to diversify its economy and to search for alternative sources of revenues should the more pessimistic forecasts hold true. It is hoped that this volume will therefore not only prove instrumental to the interested reader and specialist, but that it also will assist GCC countries design effective policies aimed at meeting future challenges.

CHAPTER I

The Role of the Gulf in World Energy: Lessons from the Past

Paul Stevens

This chapter is an attempt to assess the impact of energy exports from the Gulf on the global energy market since 1945.' It is written specifically from the perspective of the Gulf. It seeks to assess how far the exports in one period, through their effects on the global energy market, actually created feedback loops which in turn affected Gulf exports in later periods. In particular, it seeks to identify "mistakes" which arguably have been associated with the development of Gulf oil exports and which led to unwanted or undesirable consequences.' This is done not in a spirit of seeking to apportion blame, but in the spirit of Otto von Bismarck's characteristically modest maxim – "only a fool learns from his mistakes. I learn from other people's mistakes." Hopefully, by understanding the past, the chapter will set the scene to consider the future of Gulf oil exports.

To understand the role of Gulf oil exports in the world market, it is first necessary to develop an economic framework to explain how the international oil market has worked. The oil market is subject to a great variety of complex driving forces. Economic analysis can provide a framework which generates a clear agenda for discussion of these forces, including areas ranging from technology to politics. Having made the analysis manageable, the next stage is to assess in what sense Gulf oil was different from oil in other parts of the world and how its role was different. Having established the unique nature of Gulf oil, the chapter then moves into an assessment of its development and the impact of that development on supply, industry structure, and price.

The Framework for Analysis

In order to impose order on the myriad of factors which drive the oil market, an analytical framework is required to assist the analysis. The framework,

7

based upon supply and demand curves, is briefly outlined below and is illustrated in Figure 1.1. Each component of the diagram requires elaboration.[3]

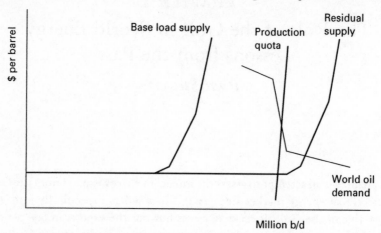

Fig. 1.1   The world oil market: a framework for analysis

The vertical axis measures a dollar crude oil price. This is a price which can
be regarded as somehow representative of "the" crude price.[4] This has
changed over time. Between 1950 and 1985 the price of Arabian Light
might suffice. Thereafter, the OPEC basket might be more representative.
The price in Figure 1.1 is given in constant 1994 dollars to allow for inflation over the period of analysis.[5] The horizontal axis measures the volume of
crude oil available or required for exchange for the most representative transaction. Again, as with price, this would change over time. Up until the second oil shock and the demise of operational vertical integration,[6] the typical
transaction would be internal deals within affiliates with relatively limited
arms-length contracts. Thereafter, arguably quarterly contracts were more
typical. The volumes are based upon a global rather than regional perspective, which is a reasonable approximation to the reality of a unified global
market.[7] Thus, the analysis is for the world oil market.[8]

The demand curve, which shows the amount of crude oil consumers are
willing and able to buy at given prices, comprises three segments. Between
a price range of $10–30 (the steeper segment of the demand curve in Figure
1.1), demand is extremely inelastic. Over a short period, change in the
demand for oil products (which underlies crude demand) can occur only as a
result of the appliance capacity utilization decision. The ability to change
utilization is limited unless conservation becomes deprivation. This inelas-
ticity is reflected in most of the empirical analyses of oil demand.[9] At much
higher prices, elasticity increases sharply as deprivation becomes forced as a

fact of economic life. At much lower prices, elasticity again might be expected to increase if there exists dual-firing capacity such as has developed since the first oil shock of 1973, notably in US manufacturing and the European power sector. Over time, the upper and lower ranges have probably been altered. For example, almost certainly during the 1950s and 1960s, the upper range would probably have been close to $20 ($3.25 in 1950). Since the oil shocks of the 1970s, many consumers have generated an ability to accommodate higher prices.[10] Economic growth, which leads to a growth in the oil-using appliance stock, means the demand curve shifts to the right; improved efficiency in the appliance stock would shift the demand curve to the left.

Global supply consists of two sections, a base load supply added to which is the residual supply.[11] The global supply curve implied in Figure 1.1 has two segments. The vertical segment reflects the constraint imposed by the availability of global capacity. It excludes capacity which may be unavailable because of wars, strikes, or legal constraints such as UN sanctions, etc. In the short run, capacity would be measured by available surge capacity. This might be sustainable for a month or so but would then be reduced if long-term field damage in rate-sensitive fields were to be avoided. A natural process of depletion or poor maintenance would shift the vertical segment to the left. Investment to convert oil-in-place into proven reserves would shift it to the right.

The horizontal segment of the supply curve argues that in the short run, provided variable costs are covered, producers are willing and able to produce. This assumes that short-run marginal costs are extremely low and are similar throughout the world. Both are realistic assumptions. Capital intensity driven by economies of scale and technology creates very low variable costs – certainly below the $5 per barrel implied in Figure 1.1. Also, the components of these costs are broadly similar irrespective of location.[12] This supply curve also assumes that producers ignore user cost and are not influenced by expectations regarding future prices. Again, this is not an unreasonable assumption in the real world. Very few governments have the financial flexibility to postpone production in anticipation of higher prices. Politicians' discount rates are simply too high. Arguably, only in the few years immediately after the first oil shock did a few governments have such an embarrassment of riches that they closed in capacity on the grounds that "oil in the ground was worth more than money in the bank."[13] Equally, while oil companies may delay development investment of known oil-in-place in a capital constrained world or in a world where they already have more producing capacity than they can use, once the investment has been made, cash 'flow requirements will invariably override price expectations.[14]

Figure 1.1 is drawn to indicate the existence of excess capacity to produce crude oil. This is a situation which has normally characterized the international industry. Since 1945, only on three occasions has the industry had no available excess capacity: 1) during the Arab oil embargo of 1973;[15] 2) during the Iranian oil workers' strike and its aftermath (including the Iraqi invasion of Iran); and, finally, 3) during the Iraqi invasion of Kuwait in 1990. The reasons for the existence of excess capacity are outlined in this author's "A Survey of Structural Change in the International Oil Industry 1945–1984".[16] However, the main explanation (to be developed below) lies in the incentive to invest in capacity while the arms-length price of crude exceeds the replacement cost of developing proven reserves.

If this excess capacity were to be produced, the result would be a price war and consequent price collapse. Hence, suppliers in Figure 1.1 are divided into two groups – base load suppliers and residual suppliers. The distinction concerns their role in the marketplace. Base load suppliers take the going price and supply to their capacity. The residual supplier constrains capacity to try and create a production quota within range of the demand curve.[17] Without this restraint embodied in the production quota line,[18] competition would push the price down to equilibrium – somewhere around $5 per barrel. Since 1945, it has been the Gulf which has dominated this residual supply role. Before the early 1970s, this was under the control and direction of the major oil companies. During the 1970s, it was largely Saudi Arabia which fulfilled the residual role based upon market information provided by the companies.[19] Since 1982, this role has been performed with various degrees of cohesion and effectiveness by OPEC, but again with the Gulf effectively dominating.[20]

Before the second oil shock, the major oil companies had excellent information regarding the oil market. This derived from their operationally vertically integrated structure and their horizontally integrated operations through their joint ownership of much of the supply. They knew fairly accurately where the world was on the demand curve and so could match their production quota lines accordingly. They knew pretty well how much oil was above ground, where it was, and where it was going. In such a world, the curves were distinct lines. All the companies had to do to make the price and defend it was to ensure that demand and production were close enough to maintain a surface tension which would support a price to clear the market.[21]

In this sense, the residual suppliers were price-makers orchestrating the market to achieve specific price goals.[22] To be sure, in the 20 years before 1970 the companies' role was neither easy nor entirely successful. The growing number of suppliers outside the control mechanisms of the residual suppliers which emerged during the 1960s put the system under strain, which was reflected in a decline in realized prices.[23] This high-quality information about the market should have disappeared following the takeover of the operating companies during the early 1970s. However, it did not. For the most part, the oil companies retained their marketing role on behalf of the governments.[24] *De facto* operational vertical integration remained intact and with it the information about supply and demand.

After the second oil shock, fundamental changes occurred in the market related to competition and market information and the crude market became progressively more competitive. There were more players in the market as new suppliers emerged in response to the oil shocks of the 1970s.[25] There was also a move away from long-term sales contracts following their discrediting during 1979–81.[26] Greater reliance on spot and short-term contracts increased the number of transactions. Increased competition also followed moves by commercial companies away from operational vertical integration to a greater use of markets. Less crude moving through inter-affiliate channels increased arms-length transactions. This increase in transactions was reinforced as oil markets began to develop forward and futures contracts. For the first time paper barrel trading emerged.[27]

There was also much greater transparency of contract terms. More transactions increased the pool of information from which the specialized agencies reported. The development of forward and futures markets, something unknown in oil before 1980, also helped. For the first time, price data were collected as a statistical record rather than trawled by the agencies. Finally, the information technology revolution made this greater information available to all at a glance on a screen.

However, a reverse transparency process began as a result of changes in the nature of market information. *Force majeure* and the takeover of marketing by governments in 1979–80, described earlier, destroyed much operational vertical integration. The result was that the information was lost to all. There were too many diverse suppliers to be sure how much oil was above ground and, more importantly, where it was going. Demand numbers were lagged and often inaccurate, requiring revision. Stock data were equally problematic. Thus, anyone who is trying to control the market, as in the old days, would have great difficulty in knowing where to place the production quota line. Also, if the residual suppliers were prone to cheating, the production quota line would often diverge from where it had been set.[28]

The demand curve and the production quota line in Figure 1.1 became fuzzy and indistinct. In this world of fuzzy curves, within a wide range, the concept of an equilibrium price which clears the market becomes irrelevant. Even the

Olympians can no longer observe small imbalances in the market. This raises a crucial question as to what determines market price, assuming the range-maker has made the range. In standard supply and demand analysis, the market is always in disequilibrium groping towards an equilibrium price. It is market imbalances which drive price movements. However, these imbalances are assumed to be observable by the market participants. If imbalances are unclear as in Figure 1.1, with fuzzy lines over a wide range of prices, price determination is essentially concerned with the belief of traders, and the belief of traders about the belief of other traders. In the words of Keynes – "anticipating what average opinion expects the average opinion to be."[29] The price remains the price only so long as market participants believe it to be the price.

In the post-1986 world, the price-making role of the residual supplier was effectively dropped. In its place, the controllers of the excess capacity – OPEC but with the Gulf still dominating – became range-makers. Their function was to try to get the production quota line close to the demand curve. The price was then set by a large number of buyers and sellers in the market, based upon belief. Given this framework for analysis, the role of Gulf oil exports since 1945 can be examined.

The Entry of Gulf Oil Exports and Their Special Characteristics

Gulf Oil was special. In the early days,[30] the oil-in-place had certain characteristics which made it unique. First, the amounts of oil-in-place were huge. Furthermore, this potential became increasingly apparent after 1945 when the rather tentative exploration efforts of the pre-war moved up a gear.[31] This domination can be seen from Figure 1.2. In addition, because of the onshore location close to deep water, the size of the fields and their geology, the oil-in-place was extremely cheap to produce compared to the rest of the world.[32] Figures 1.3 and 1.4 illustrate the point for 1955 and 1985. Third, the central location of the Gulf, lying between the markets of East and West, meant significant market opportunities. This was reinforced as the cost of ocean transport of crude fell, reflecting the increasing absorption of economies of scale into the tanker fleet. Table 1.1 illustrates this point. Market access was also reinforced by the growth in the tanker fleet clearly seen in Figure 1.5. As output grew, the means to get it to market at ever lower freight rates also grew. Finally, Gulf oil was special because of the concession structure of joint ventures. This meant that the growing capacity in the Gulf was jointly controlled by the major oil companies, as can be seen in Figure 1.6. This joint ownership in part reflected the role of the major powers in allocating concessions in the pre-war period.[33] However, it also

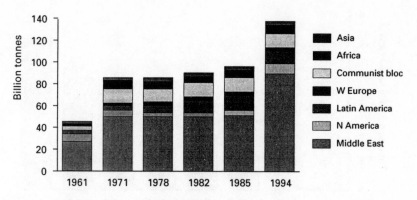

Note: The Middle East can be taken as the Gulf.

Source: BP, annual; OPEC, Statistical Bulletin, 1994.

Fig. 1.2   The role of Gulf oil in world oil reserves

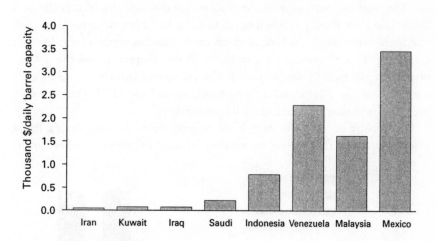

Source: Adelman and Shahi, 1989.

Fig. 1.3   Development operating costs, selected countries, 1955

reflected a growing awareness of what was to become the central problem associated with Gulf oil exports. How were such large amounts of extremely cheap oil to be brought into the international system without the sort of price wars which had characterized the international industry before the 1928 Achnacarry agreement? One solution was for crude long companies to enter joint ventures with crude short companies allowing them access to the

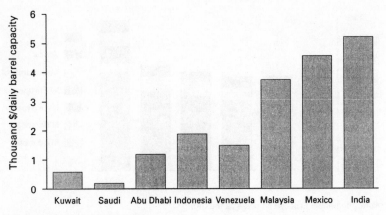

Fig. 1.4   Development operating costs, selected countries, 1985

oil. This had two virtues. First, it enabled the development of capacity at a faster rate than if only crude long companies had been in control. Second, and more importantly, it dissuaded the crude short companies from looking elsewhere. To anticipate a key conclusion of this chapter, it was the neglect of this virtue, first by the majors in the 1960s and then by the Gulf governments in the 1970s and 1980s, which caused the Gulf exporters such problems and now threatens their future markets.

The starting point of the story is the opening up of the Gulf Basing Point pricing system.[34] This system meant that products imported anywhere in the

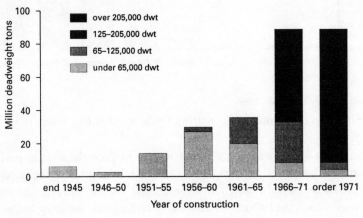

Fig. 1.5   Additions to the world tanker fleet, 1945–71

world from any source were priced as though the products had been brought and shipped from the Gulf of Mexico. Differences were made up by the addition of a phantom freight rate. Such an approach, which was a key part of the Achnacarry system, effectively restrained the entry of low-cost crude sources. At some point during the Second World War,[35] following pressure from both the British and US Navies, Abadan in the Gulf was allowed as a second basing point. From then, although the FOB price was still based upon the Gulf of Mexico price,[36] the freight rate became real rather than phantom.

Table 1.1   The cost of crude oil transportation

Freight cost – percent of cif price	Freight cost: Gulf-US East Coast $/barrel	Crude price fob $/barrel	
54.6	1.73	1.44	1952
27.2	0.92	2.47	1972
3.7	1.11	29.00	1984

Source: Derived from data in Adelman, 1972 and Zannetos, 1987

This was the absolutely crucial change for Gulf oil exports. Immediately, the oil had its own market within watersheds defined by the relative costs of transport from the Gulf compared to the Gulf of Mexico. By the end of the 1940s, the Western watershed became the US East Coast. This process of expanding the Gulf's market was slowed as companies tried desperately to maintain the link between FOB prices in the United States and the Gulf. When this failed,[37] the door was completely opened for the Gulf to benefit from its low cost of production. The consequences of these changes were enormous in terms of their impact on supply, industry structure, and prices. Each will now be considered.

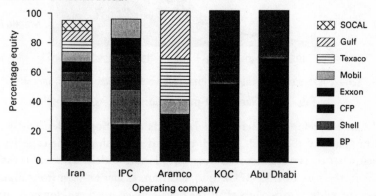

Fig. 1.6   Joint control of Gulf oil supplies

The Impact of Gulf Oil Exports

Supply

In terms of the framework, the role of the Gulf becomes apparent. Following the Marshall Plan, the post-war period saw an economic boom of unprecedented dimensions with the result that oil demand was growing rapidly.[38] Hence, the demand curve was shifting rapidly to the right. Rising demand required rising supply and the low-cost resources of the Gulf provided the obvious source. Furthermore, the capacity could be brought onstream quickly as demand grew. The loss of Iranian supplies following the 1951 nationalization, for example, was barely noticed as new capacity in Kuwait and Iraq was developed.[39] Thus, the vertical segment of the supply curve could more than match the rightward shift of the demand curve.

Two results followed. First, increasing amounts of Gulf oil were supplied until they came to dominate the international market, as can be seen from Figure 1.7. Second, the Gulf became increasingly used as the shelf inventory for the international industry. Thus, as can be seen from Figure 1.7, fluctuations in world demand were for the most part absorbed by Gulf capacity. Two reasons explain this role in the years up to the 1970s. First, such capacity was

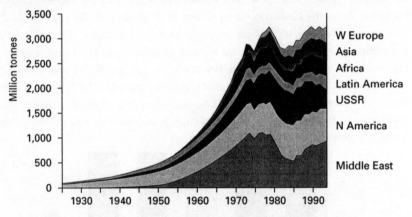

Source: 1925–60 Darmstadter et al., 1971; 1965–94 *BP Statistical Review*, annual.

Fig. 1.7   World oil production 1925–94, by region

cheap to develop and therefore delaying its utilization was less costly than in other parts of the world. Second, the joint ownership of the capacity meant that what costs were incurred were spread more widely. This was most apparent in the case of Iraq (IPC). Iraq and Iran, as can be seen from Figure 1.6, had the widest ownership of all the operating companies. However, attitudes towards the two ruling regimes differed significantly. Iran was increasingly

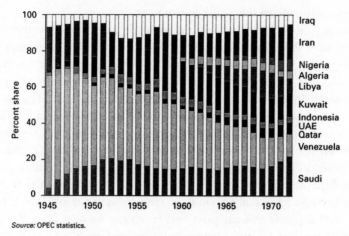

Source: OPEC statistics.

Fig. 1.8 Iraq as shelf inventory

seen as the key ally in US regional policy while Iraq was seen as an awkward, potentially disruptive factor after the 1958 revolution. The result was that Iraq became the key residual supplier.[40] Other Gulf countries still played a partial role in orchestrating supply but their role lay in slower rather than faster capacity expansion. As can be seen from Figure 1.8, Iraq became the real shelf inventory for the industry. If the market looked oversupplied, a dispute could be manufactured. If the market looked like tightening, negotiating postures could be relaxed.

This control over the expansion and utilization of Gulf capacity disappeared between 1972 and 1976 as the Gulf governments took over the operating companies either through nationalization or creeping "participation."[41] Thus, the decision over how much capacity to install and how much to produce passed directly to the governments. During the 1970s, the amount of excess capacity in the world oil market declined. Demand growth had increased dramatically in the period between 1969 and 1973 as the world experienced a boom and low price expectations dominated the late 1960s. The demand curve had moved sharply to the right. The announcement of "participation" by Zaki Yamani in 1967–68,[42] led to a moratorium in capacity expansion by the oil companies. Hence, the supply curve ceased to track demand's rightward shift. A number of suppliers, notably Kuwait and Libya, actually closed in capacity either because of concerns about over-production and field damage or in anticipation of higher prices. Thus, the amount of excess capacity to control was diminished and it fell mainly to Saudi Arabia to act as the residual supplier. This was not an especially arduous task since it required a genuine swing role with production fluctuating around an output level acceptable to the Saudi government.

Following the second oil shock, the oil market changed dramatically. The demand curve shifted to the left, reflecting a combination of recession, fuel switching, and conservation. The latter two factors began to appear after the first oil shock of 1973. The moves were triggered partly by higher oil prices,[43] but above all by expectations of yet higher prices to come. The base load supply at the same time began to move rapidly to the right, reflecting the frantic search for oil which followed the exclusion of the companies from the low-cost supplies of the Gulf and the expectation of ever higher prices. Given the growing size of excess capacity, Saudi Arabia alone as residual supplier was insufficient to maintain surface tension and in 1982, for the first time, OPEC introduced a formal system to set the production quota line. It became the residual supplier and the price-maker. As can be seen from Figure 1.7, much of the reduction in demand required came from the Gulf, with Saudi Arabia bearing the greatest drop. In effect, Saudi Arabia took over Iraq's position as shelf inventory within the residual supply role and suffered as Iraq had done.

The significance of the events of 1985, when Saudi Arabia gave up the swing role and announced netback pricing, was that this effectively killed the price-making role. OPEC subsequently became only the range-maker, with price determination being left to an increasingly competitive (if poorly informed) market. The system muddled along until the Iraqi invasion of Kuwait and the subsequent imposition of sanctions at a stroke removed the excess capacity. The vertical part of the supply line and the production quota line coincided. Following the liberation of Kuwait, only Saudi Arabia has any significant amounts of excess capacity.[44] Thus, it is primarily Saudi Arabia which is now the range-maker and appears willing and able to maintain that role. Iraq, however, has been returned to its shelf inventory role, although it must be said that US insistence on sanctions has everything to do with US domestic political considerations and nothing to do with oil.[45]

One dimension of the Gulf supply role, concerning exports of crude versus those of products, should be mentioned. Prior to the Second World War, most refineries were located on the oil fields reflecting high processing losses and a highly unbalanced demand barrel. During the 1950s, a reverse trend began to develop, as can be seen from Figure 1.9. This was in response to reduced process losses, a demand barrel almost exactly matching the simple yield from Arabian Light, a desire to save foreign exchange, and concern over nationalization. Hence, the dramatic increase in oil exports from the Gulf which began in the 1950s concerned crude only. Following the first oil shock, some Gulf governments, by virtue of their newly acquired right of crude

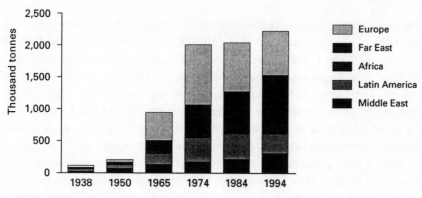

Source: Crook, 1975 and BP, annual.

Fig. 1.9   Refining outside communist bloc and North America

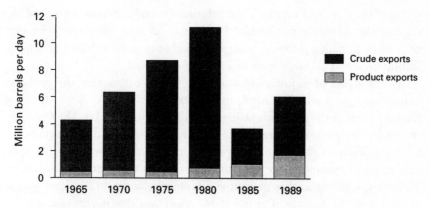

Source: OPEC, Statistical Bulletin, 1994.

Fig. 1.10   Saudi Arabia and Kuwait, 1965–89: oil exports by type

disposal and their surplus revenues, began to consider developing export refinery capacity. The wisdom of these plans was and is debatable.[46] In the event, many were shelved and only Saudi Arabia developed significant primary distillation capacity for export.[47] As can be seen from Figure 1.10, the result was a steady growth in the proportion of oil exported as products. A tempting conclusion to be drawn from Figure 1.10 is that product exports, unlike crude exports, exhibited stable growth and avoided the volatility of crude exports.[48] However, to extrapolate to the argument that investment in more downstream capacity would reduce volume volatility might be dangerous and would require significant elaboration.

Industry structure

In terms of the analytical framework, the structure of the industry is relevant in terms of the concentration of supply. There are two dimensions. First, is the size and the concentration of the base load supply compared to total demand. The larger the number of suppliers outside of the residual suppliers "club", the poorer the market information will be. Second, there is the dimension of how many are involved as residual suppliers. Other things being equal, the more residual suppliers there are, the greater is the probability of conflicting interests, poor cohesion, and generally weak control.

During the 1950s and 1960s, the proportion of residual supply was smaller compared to the 1980s. Between 1965 and 1970, the Gulf (as base load supplier) accounted on average for 33.3 percent of non-communist demand while during 1982–89 the base load supplier (now OPEC) accounted on average for 44 percent. However, in the 1960s, the controllers (i.e., the majors) were working towards the same objectives. They also controlled much of the base load supply. Thus, information and cohesion were good and control was relatively successful.[19] In contrast, in the 1980s, the controllers were often pursuing different goals and could only guess at base load supply. Information and cohesion were bad and control failed.

To this aspect of industry structure, the Gulf, both during the period of majors' and government control, made a crucial contribution which lies at the very heart of the problems facing the Gulf producers today. The Gulf producers by their actions as residual supplier have supported and protected a price significantly above the cost of replacing proven reserves. Thus, by their actions they created the incentive for oil companies to invest in new capacity. Yet, at the same time, they prevented oil company access to the development of their own oil-in-place. The inevitable result was that higher cost reserves outside of the Gulf were developed in response to the economic incentives created by the action of the Gulf producers. Base load supply therefore increased, the Gulf lost out on the growth in volume, and the extent of excess capacity to control grew to unmanageable levels. They found themselves having to exercise ever greater restraint to maintain the price from which other owners of oil-in-place benefited. The action by the Gulf producers significantly reduced supply concentration in the industry by increasing the number of suppliers. If the oil companies had had open access to Gulf oil-in-place, given its significantly lower costs, much of the rise in non-Gulf supplies seen since the late 1950s would not have happened.

During the 1950s and 1960s, these restrictions on access were imposed by the companies. The various lifting arrangements in the operating companies such as APQ in Iran, Five-Sevenths in Iraq, and others, made overlifting expensive.[50] Hence, crude short companies began to develop alternative acreage outside the Gulf.[51] Similarly, newcomers to the market, notably the US independents, attracted by the much higher profitability of Eastern Hemisphere operations, were prevented from gaining acreage in the Gulf and went elsewhere.[52] The result, as can be seen from Figure 1.11, was a weakening of supply concentration in the 1960s. In 1950, the eight majors owned 100 percent of production outside of the United States and the communist bloc. By 1969, this had fallen to 80 percent.

This process of developing capacity outside of the Gulf accelerated dramatically following Zaki Yamani's announcement of "participation" during 1967–68.[53] At this point, investment in further capacity in the Gulf virtually ceased and resources were redirected to alternative acreage. Following the takeover of the operating companies in the Gulf between 1972 and 1976, the

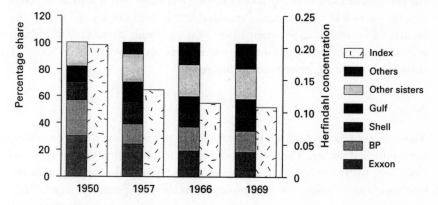

Source: Adelman, 1972.

Fig. 1.11   "Ownership" of WOCANA production 1950–69, by company

doors to foreign company access were closed tightly. This was entirely understandable. In those heady days of the successful assertion of national sovereignty it would have been inconceivable to allow foreign company entry. However, the result was a dramatic increase in the development of capacity elsewhere, as can be seen from Figure 1.7. Hence, the base load supply curve shifted inexorably to the right, absorbing the rightward shift in the demand curve.[54] The residual supplier was faced with increasing amounts of excess capacity from which to pluck the production quota and make the range. The more successful the Gulf (and OPEC generally) were in maintaining price above reserve replacement costs, the more they were digging their own graves while they refused access to their oil-in-place.[55]

The result has been a gross underdevelopment of Gulf oil reserves. In 1993, the reserve production ratio of the world outside of the Gulf was 20.7 years. If such a ratio were to be applied to the Gulf, assuming no investment constraints, the Gulf could support a production of 88 million b/d. Production in 1994 was 19 million b/d. More recently, there have been signs of change. With the notable exception of Saudi Arabia, all the countries of the region are now seeking foreign company involvement to find and/or develop their oil-in-place. The most interesting example is likely to be post-sanctions Iraq, where there is a large undeveloped oil-in-place which could be brought onstream very quickly.

Another impact on industry structure derived from the Arab Gulf exporters concerns the institutional arrangements between the owner of the oil and the operator. This is a complex story and space precludes its development here. However, the role of the region's producers in the development of the concept of joint ventures and in the development and spread of the concept of "participation" has been considerable.[56] It might be argued that in the future, more imaginative arrangements for upstream development linking into downstream partnership to secure market access – Yamani's "catholic marriage" – could generate interesting results.

Prices

The contribution of Arab Gulf oil exports to pricing has, to a large extent, been outlined earlier. The Gulf producers were at the forefront of negotiations over fiscal terms during the 1960s and have played a major role in the determination of prices.[57] For example, it was the Gulf producers, not OPEC, who announced the rise in price in October 1973.[58] By controlling their own capacity and acting as residual supplier, either alone or with other members of OPEC, they have protected price. Between 1950 and 1986, the Gulf producers acted as price-makers. Since 1986, however, they have been relegated to range-makers, with prices being made by the market. As can be seen from Figure 1.12, in general, they have been successful in both roles, although for how much longer is a matter for debate.[59]

However, apart from their control of the actual mechanics of residual supply, Arab Gulf oil exports have played another role in oil prices through their impact on expectations. The history of the oil industry shows that price expectations are crucial. Supply and demand do not respond significantly to high or low prices. What they do respond to is price expectations. The fuel switching and the conservation experienced in the 1970s and 1980s were driven by the belief that oil prices would go on rising forever. The same is

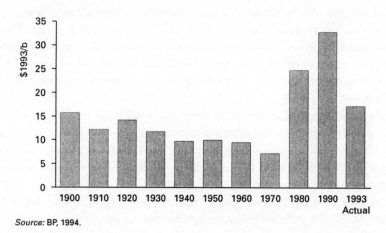

Source: BP, 1994.

Fig. 1.12   Average oil prices, 1900–93 (always of the preceding ten years)

true of rising capacity. In terms of the framework, it is price expectations which can shift the curves.

The Gulf has played a central role in influencing market expectations. At times this role has had a negative effect on the Gulf's own market prospects. Consumers, rightly or wrongly, perceive the Gulf to be an unstable region. This has prompted consumer governments to take a succession of measures to reduce dependence on imported oil in general and Gulf oil in particular. Furthermore, over time, these measures have increasingly been regarded as acceptable by those voting for consumer governments. This has been reinforced to some extent by the ability of the politicians to wrap up many of these measures of protection in a cloak of environmental concern.[60]

The result is that over the years, essentially protectionist measures which would normally attract considerable opposition have become respectable and acceptable in the consumer countries. Every war or rumor of war in the Gulf has reinforced this tendency and will continue to do so.

Conclusions

The Arab Gulf oil exporters have played a key role in the world energy markets since 1945. They have had a significant impact on supply, making available large amounts of low-cost energy to feed the world's insatiable appetite for energy as an input into the process of growth and development. They have also played crucial roles in influencing the structure of the international industry and the price at which oil is traded. However, increasingly this role has embodied a fundamental contradiction. On the one hand their role as residual supplier protected prices from competition thereby creating incentives to develop capacity. On the other hand, by restricting access, they allowed other owners of oil-in-place to gain the benefit. The result is a self-destructive process whereby the more successful the control of prices, the more difficult it becomes to control prices as new sources of oil marginalize Gulf reserves.

At the moment, it may appear to many that Gulf oil is the only possible source of energy to meet the growing demands of the world, especially the developing world.[61] Thus, so the argument goes, there is an inevitability about a rising demand for Gulf oil. The history of the role of Gulf oil exporters in the industry since 1945 suggests that this may not be the case. The role played has created serious challenges in the form of alternative supplies of energy and growing measures by consumers to constrain markets.

CHAPTER 2

A Relevant Framework for Understanding the Global Crude Oil Market

Vahan Zanoyan

Introduction

This chapter is concerned with the commercial and economic fundamentals of the global crude oil market. The emphasis is on the key forces that shape market realities in the short to medium term. The commercial forces that influence the global crude oil market have gained clear precedence not only over the institutional forces, but also over political considerations that may have overwhelmed the market during the Cold War years. More than ever before, at the level of daily market trends, trade patterns, and short-term price determination, the global oil game is a commercial game.

However, before delving into a discussion of the economic fundamentals, it should be stressed that a number of critical structural shifts in the global oil market provide the broad context within which this chapter endeavors to construct an analytical framework. These shifts, which will not be discussed in any detail but will be assumed and taken for granted throughout the chapter, can be summarized as follows.

There has been a clear trend in the past ten to fifteen years whereby some of the lowest-cost producing areas cut down production, while relatively high-cost producing areas have raised production to full capacity. Until around five years ago, when the low-cost producers were also the main marginal (residual) suppliers, this did not represent a fundamental challenge to them. However, in the past few years, the higher-cost producers have become the main incremental suppliers of crude oil. The key forces that have made this possible are, first, the vast revenue needs of the governments of the low-cost producing areas, which have created a huge gap between the price level at which the national oil company covers all of its costs and the price level which balances the overall government budget; and second, the technologi-

cal advances that have driven down production costs in the high-cost producing areas. As long as these forces remain in effect, the higher-cost
producers could remain the incremental suppliers. This does pose a major
problem to the low-cost producers, not only because it leads to the much
publicized losses in market share, but also, and much more seriously, because
it further undermines their ability to meet their overall revenue needs.

The policy dilemma that this situation presents to the governments of the
low-cost producing areas, especially those in the Gulf, is formidable. While
a continuation of recent trends in market share could be disastrous in the
long term, any attempt to recapture lost market share carries with it enormous short-term financial risks. The fact that either option could lead to an
untenable situation underscores the most significant problem with the
current structure of oil markets.

This chapter will revolve around the following four different but related
themes: *First, the question of how to best organize the physical world for purposes of
analyzing the global crude oil market.* Supply–demand balances and trade patterns in oil do not conform to boundaries fashioned by the Cold War mind-
set. The "OPEC versus non-OPEC" way of thinking about crude oil supplies
persists in spite of the fact that it is not very useful to understanding either
current supply trends or future supply potential. The "OECD versus non-
OECD" way of thinking about demand has also lost considerable relevance,
and yet remains widespread. The dominance of these institutions, and the
legacy of the institutional way of thinking about market fundamentals that
became fashionable in the 1970s, have helped prolong conventional but
increasingly irrelevant ways of thinking and methods of analysis about the
global oil market. It is much more useful to focus on the actual patterns of
trade among key exporting and importing geographic regions and on the
main economic growth centers in the world, regardless of whether they fall
into the OPEC or OECD camps.

The second theme is the question of an appropriate time structure for analysis.
Another methodological convention that has lost some relevance is related to
the time structure used in analyzing market fundamentals – neither the quarterly structure of supply–demand balances, nor some of the conventional
assumptions about seasonal patterns in demand are particularly useful when
it comes to understanding the global crude oil market. While product markets are still subject to the seasonal pattern dictated by swings in final
demand, crude oil markets have become increasingly immune for seasonality.
The timing of refinery turnarounds and the schedules for crude oil field
maintenance and shutdowns are much more relevant determinants of short-
term market fundamentals.

The third theme will be the changing role of governments in the global crude oil fundamentals. The conventional way of analyzing the global crude oil market generally fails to give adequate recognition to the changing role of governments, budgetary pressures, and macro-economic constraints in the formulation of both short-term and long-term oil policy. As a host of economic, financial, and, in some cases, political problems surfaced with new intensity and seriousness in various oil- and gas-producing countries, the internal conditions in these countries came under closer scrutiny. Very few oil exporting countries enjoy the financial cushion that they had a few years ago. The economic and financial consequences of short-term oil policy decisions of the key producers, not only for their own economies, but also for those of other exporting countries, have become much more immediate and profound than they were a few years ago. Moreover, domestic financial constraints remain the most credible hurdle facing long-term capacity expansion plans and prospects, especially in countries that do not allow private sector investment in the oil and gas sector.

Fourth, the chapter will briefly discuss the proliferation of futures and forward markets and the nature of the various players in that area. As recently as several years ago, it would have been acceptable to exclude paper markets from a discussion of market fundamentals. Wet barrels and paper barrels were treated as different commodities, with traders in one generally having little to do with traders in the other. Today, that distinction would be largely artificial. Many participants in physical markets – producers, refiners, and traders – are also engaged in paper markets, creating a gray area of overlapping activity, which has become part of the global market fundamentals.

Institutional Versus Geographic Regions

Patterns of crude oil production and trade in the world evolve subject to underlying commercial, physical, and technical constraints, opportunities, and motives. Institutional concepts – such as OPEC production or OPEC's share in world output – do not have much operational significance. Ten years ago, when OPEC maintained over 11 million b/d of excess capacity and when virtually every member of the organization was producing below its capacity, the concept of "OPEC market share" had some significance for policy within the organization. Today, when the organization's excess capacity is not more than 2.5 to 3 million b/d (excluding Iraq) and when most members are already producing at full capacity, the concept is void of any policy significance. The commercial dimension of the global hydrocarbon sector is no longer overwhelmed by its political dimension. Market share itself is not a

political issue. It cannot be resolved by political means. One cannot "negoti-
ate" market share with fellow producing countries, whether in or out of
OPEC. It is a commercial and economic issue and can be dealt with only
through commercially meaningful policies – having to do with locking-in
markets, either through joint ventures and other asset acquisition schemes,
or through long-term supply arrangements that have intrinsic value to certain customers.

Individual countries, both within and out of OPEC, have managed to raise
their market share in recent years for reasons specific to them and to their
niche markets. Venezuela is an excellent example. Venezuela's first priority is
to secure North America as its natural niche market. The commercial factors
driving this policy have basically overwhelmed whatever leftover political
factors might still be lingering in the Venezuelan policy-makers' minds
about OPEC and cohesion within its ranks. The world has changed, OPEC
has changed and, from a Venezuelan perspective, the Gulf members of OPEC
and Saudi Arabia in particular have done extremely well in enhancing their
market share in the past four years.

Many producing countries – including members of OPEC – are opening
up their upstream to foreign participation. This is not only another part of
the Venezuelan story, but is true also in Algeria and even in Libya. Algeria is
on the verge of raising its output substantially, Venezuela will soon move to
3 million b/d. Libya, once sanctions are lifted, could move from about 1.4
million b/d to close to 2 million b/d. Quota agreements with OPEC will play
a secondary role in these countries' production decisions. The traditional way
of dealing with them through intra-OPEC haggling will not be effective and
could be counterproductive in terms of depressing oil prices. OPEC members
that currently maintain excess capacity in order to adhere to their quotas –
basically Saudi Arabia and, to a much lesser extent, Kuwait and the United
Arab Emirates – will clearly resent this trend.

Another supply side issue that has changed in the OPEC/non-OPEC
dynamic in the past several years is the changing role of various producers as
marginal suppliers of crude oil. The most important supply-side variable
influencing the price of oil is the *change in marginal supplies*. The last barrel of
oil that is either added to or subtracted from the flow of total supply exerts
more pressure on oil prices than the entire base flow itself. Thus, it is generally less important whether total world output on a given day is running at,
say, 68.1 mmb/d or 68.4 mmb/d, than whether it *changed* by 300,000 b/d.

Judged from this vantage point, the producing regions with most
influence on oil price trends in the last few years have been the North Sea
and, to a lesser extent, the Former Soviet Union (FSU). Figure 2.1 demon-

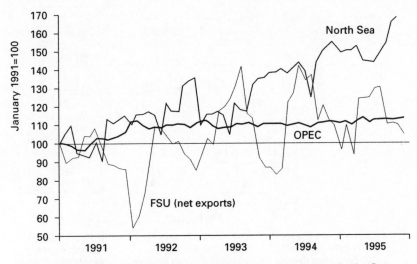

Source: January 1991–July 1995: index constructed based on historical production figures from *Petroleum Intelligence Weekly.* Projections are from Petro Finance.

Fig. 2.1   Monthly OPEC and North Sea crude oil output and net exports from the FSU (index, January 1991 = 100; January 1991–December 1995)

strates this point. OPEC production has remained remarkably constant during the past four years, while wide fluctuations in North Sea output and in net exports from the FSU have determined the direction of marginal supplies and consequently short-term fluctuations in oil prices. Thus, OPEC's role in influencing short-term oil price movements has been reduced considerably, leading to a de-politicization of short-term oil markets.' This has brought the market fundamentals and other commercial factors into sharper focus.

If the OPEC/non-OPEC framework is less relevant for crude oil supplies and trade patterns, then what is more relevant? A more realistic and accurate approach is to divide the world into commercially relevant geographic regions and to analyze the production and trade patterns in and between those regions. Taking account of a host of considerations, including production patterns, export patterns, tanker route considerations, crude oil quality, demand patterns, refinery complexity, geographic and geopolitical issues, and data considerations, it is possible to identify fourteen commercially relevant regions. These are depicted in Figure 2.2. The crude export streams of most of these regions have a consistent quality – with over 75 percent of the Mediterranean export flows being sweet light crudes, over 85 percent of the Gulf being sour crudes, almost 82 percent of the flows from Northwest

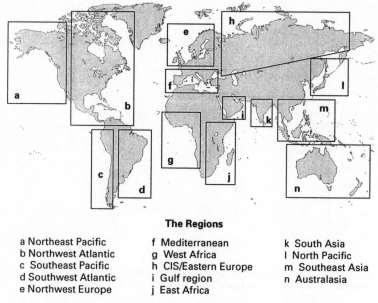

The Regions

a Northeast Pacific	f Mediterranean	k South Asia
b Northwest Atlantic	g West Africa	l North Pacific
c Southeast Pacific	h CIS/Eastern Europe	m Southeast Asia
d Southwest Atlantic	i Gulf region	n Australasia
e Northwest Europe	j East Africa	

Fig. 2.2   The commercially relevant regions

Europe being sweet light crudes, etc. These and other regional crude oil export streams are depicted in Figure 2.3.

Not only are the current flows from each region dominated by a specific crude quality, but also the expected changes in the next five to ten years will have a pattern that fits this regional breakdown. Production of light liquids will increase in the North Sea and output of light sweet crudes will rise in Colombia and West Africa. Although limited additions of light and sweet crude streams are expected in the Gulf, the balance will remain clearly sour. Additionally, close to a million b/d of heavy crude is expected from Venezuela and the Gulf of Mexico.

These regions also display distinct patterns of refinery complexity and therefore of demand for different grades of crude oil. Figure 2.4 summarizes the average refinery complexity in each region.[2] Sophisticated refineries in the US West Coast and in the Northwest Atlantic can handle heavier and more sour crudes than those in South Asia, West Africa and the FSU; in the North Pacific, there is more desulfurization capacity than upgrading capacity, implying larger demand for light sour grades of crude oil.

Clearly, the combination of the two patterns – i.e., that of crude quality of export flows, which determine the supply side, and refinery complexity, which determines the demand side – sets the pattern of world trade. And as the crude oil quality streams and refinery configurations around the world

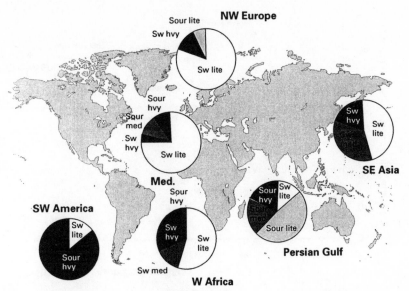

Source: Petroleum Finance Company, Long-Term Workshop.

Fig. 2.3 Quality of crude export streams, 1994

change, so will trade patterns. Interestingly, even when indigenous production in a net importing region rises, it does not necessarily mean that gross imports into that region will decline. Depending on the quality of crude oil produced in the region and on requirements elsewhere, trade in crude oil might actually increase, while *net* imports into the region decline.

Refiners around the world will continue to add upgrading and desulfurization capacity, but important regional differences will remain in refining complexity as well as in the structure of final demand. For example, in the Asia/Pacific region, more desulfurization capacity than upgrading is likely to be added in the next five to seven years, while the reverse is true in the Atlantic Basin. In Asia, the combination of trends in the quality of crude oil supplies and refining complexity imply an increase in demand for light crudes (see Figure 2.5).

Aside from indigenous production and refinery complexity, a number of other factors will influence the pattern of trade in crude oil globally during the next several years. Environmental and regulatory constraints will present a much more serious restriction on the addition of new refining capacity in some regions than in others, influencing the direction of future demand for crude oil. The structure of demand for final products, especially in the fast-growing regions, is also important because it changes the quality mix of the average crude oil barrel that enters into a refinery.

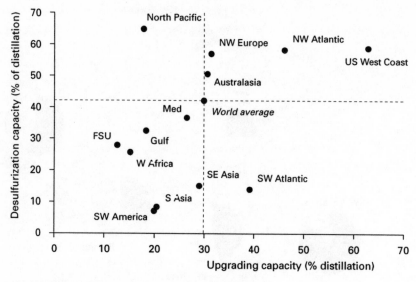

Source: Petroleum Finance Company, Long-Term Workshop.

Fig. 2.4   Quality of the world's refining capacity, 1994

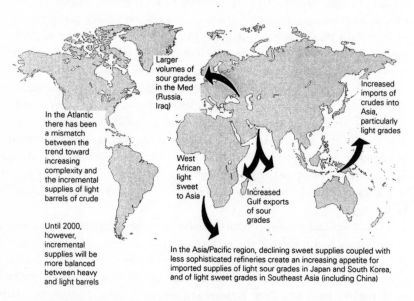

Source: Petroleum Finance Company, Long-Term Workshop.

Fig. 2.5   Changing patterns in crude supply and refiners' demand for crude: implications for sweet/sour differentials

The Time Dimension

There are two rigidities in the time structure of supply–demand analysis that do not pass the market test. One is related to the seasonality in crude oil and product markets, and the second is related to the temptation to adhere to a quarterly time structure, just because that happens to be the basis for much of the available statistical data.

The seasonality issue is crucial to understanding not only market behavior, but also the implications of specific production policies, such as the relatively constant production trend from OPEC during the past few years that was highlighted earlier. There were good reasons for OPEC to launch the constant production policy a few years ago, not the least of which was the fact that OPEC's attempts to fine-tune production to meet demand for OPEC crude on a quarterly basis were failing miserably. This result was due, in part, to grave methodological problems with OPEC's approach and in part to the fact that it is never easy to fine-tune output to match a specific trend in demand in order to defend a predetermined price level.[5]

The methodological problems were almost entirely related to a failure to distinguish between seasonal patterns in demand for products and demand for crude oil. Although final demand does demonstrate a clear and predictable seasonal pattern, refinery behavior shields crude oil markets from the seasonality of product markets. Neither the winter surge nor the spring decline in demand for products gets reflected in proportionate swings in demand for crude oil.

For example, there is a substantial drop in final demand every second quarter – amounting to roughly between 2.7 and 3.1 million b/d. But refiners do not cut their refinery runs by that volume. They continue to refine and store the additional product, which enables them not to *raise* runs later in the year, when the final demand surges. Thus, demand for crude oil does not drop by as much as demand for products in the second quarter, nor does it rise by as much in the third and fourth quarters. While demand for products continues to demonstrate a marked seasonal pattern, demand for crude oil does not. Figure 2.6 demonstrates this point.

Looking at Figure 2.6, it is easy to see how OPEC *underestimated* the demand for crude oil and consequently the call on its crude oil every second quarter, and *overestimated* both every fourth quarter. The quarterly and semi-annual quota adjustments that OPEC used to make before the constant-production policy took effect reflect these miscalculations. This in part explains the seemingly counter-intuitive pattern in oil prices in recent years – when the strongest period for crude oil prices has generally coincided with the weakest seasonal demand for products.

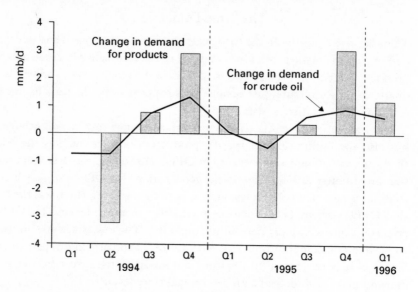

Source: Global Oil Markets, a monthly report of the Petro Finance Market Intelligence Service.

Fig. 2.6   Quarterly change in final demand versus quarterly change
in refinery runs

There are many factors that explain the behavior of refiners, the most
important of which can be summarized as follows:[4]

— Growing and increasingly transparent markets for key petroleum products, combined with more sophisticated trading and hedging practices,
have allowed refiners to take advantage of the vast opportunities provided by futures markets. These opportunities typically allow refiners to
lock in much more attractive profit margins than those afforded by contemporaneous spreads, largely due to the seasonal contangoes in product
markets (typically strong contangoes in gasoline prices in the winter, and
in distillate prices in the summer). Thus, a refiner that has already sold
forward the next season's product, continues to operate the refinery in the
low demand season and stores the product for delivery at the appropriate
time, even if contemporaneous margins are weak.

— Low storage costs (relative to the contango in product prices) have made
the rewards for sound product inventory management on the part of
refiners much more attractive. With relatively constant runs – implying
relatively constant demand for crude oil – seasonal variations in product
demand are met by corresponding variations in product stocks, leaving
the seasonal swings in crude oil stocks much flatter than those in product stocks (see Figure 2.7).

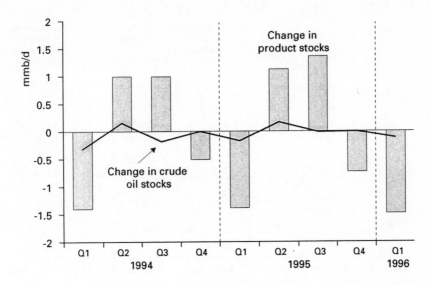

Source: Global Oil Markets, a monthly report of the Petro Finance Market Intelligence Service

Fig. 2.7   Quarterly change in product stocks versus quarterly change
in crude oil stocks

Another critical consideration in analyzing the global crude oil market is the pattern in which refiners and crude oil-producing fields in various regions start and end their maintenance programs. It is this pattern that dictates the swings in the net crude oil requirements of specific regions. Not surprisingly, this pattern does not conform to a rigid quarterly time structure. For example, net crude oil requirements in the Atlantic Basin typically surge in June–July, as refiners end their maintenance schedules and crude oil producers in the North Sea start them. In the September–October period, refiners start maintenance shutdowns again, causing a substantial drop in net crude oil requirements of the region (Figure 2.8).

It is noteworthy that the net crude oil requirements in the Asia/Pacific region, while showing partial overlap with the Atlantic Basin in *direction*, alternate between rising above the Atlantic Basin and falling behind, creating arbitrage opportunities. Generally, while net crude requirements in the Atlantic Basin rise dramatically in June, they fall in the Asia/Pacific region, and both trends reverse in July–August. Also, in the May–August period, Atlantic Basin requirements far exceed those of Asia Pacific, while in the September–May period the reverse is true.

These shifts, which do not conform to any quarterly schedule and have vir-

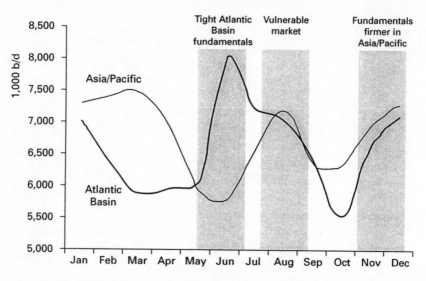

Source: Global Oil Markets, a monthly report of the Petro Finance Market Intelligence Service.

Fig. 2.8   Net crude oil requirements in the Atlantic Basin and
Asia/Pacific regions (crude oil demand less regional crude supply)

tually no way of fitting any OPEC/non-OPEC or OECD/non-OECD mold,
exert a profound influence not only on the direction of crude oil prices in specific regions, but also on the relative prices of crude oil across regions. These
factors explain, at least in part, some of the price patterns established during
the past few years. Figure 2.9 demonstrates clearly the "counter-seasonal"
decline in oil prices during the fourth quarter of every year, as well as the relative strength in the summer months – the June–August period.

Different events every year "distort" the pattern by starting trends earlier
or by exacerbating an already unfolding situation. For example, in 1994, a
series of events, including the Nigerian oil workers' strike and the civil war
in Yemen, helped add considerable momentum to the spring rally, pushing
prices well above the range that would have been achievable otherwise. In
1995, a different set of events – the August troop buildup in the Gulf, the
state of emergency in Colombia, the threat of an oil workers' strike in Brazil,
four hurricanes in the United States – combined with extremely low stock
levels in the United States, helped reverse an early August downtrend.

Figure 2.10 highlights the relationship between net crude oil import
requirements in the Atlantic Basin and the price of WTI. It is interesting to
note that both current market realities and future demand affect prices at any

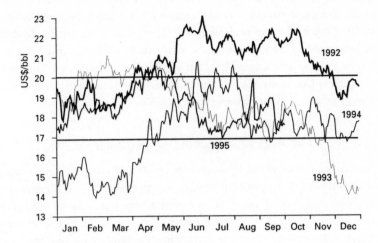

Source: Petro Finance Market Intelligence Service.

Fig. 2.9   Futures prices of WTI (daily settlement prices, US$/bbl)

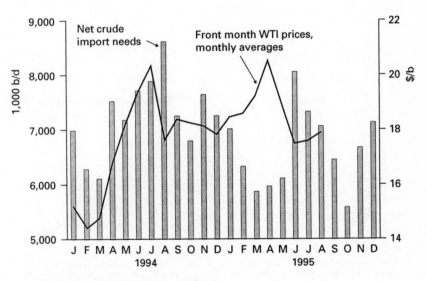

Source: Petro Finance Market Intelligence Service.

Fig. 2.10   Net crude oil import needs in the Atlantic Basin
and WTI prices

given point in time; current realities set the tone in physical markets, and buying for future months affects current prices through the demand conditions in the future. Refiners may start buying their crude oil needs two or three months prior to their peak demand. Thus, a price surge can lead the peak in net crude oil requirements by as much as three months, just as a price downturn can lead a trough in net crude oil requirements. The *combination* of these price leads and contemporaneous fundamentals is a critical determinant of prices at any given point in time.

The Role of Producing Governments

The relationship between the hydrocarbon sector and the national economy in most developing oil-producing countries has changed in a fundamental way over the past two decades. The hydrocarbon sector is no longer an exogenous sector immune from the broader economic and financial realities and pressures. More than ever, the economic constraints have become binding at all levels. Perhaps the most significant consequence of the mounting financial problems of oil-exporting countries for the global oil market is the fact that the hydrocarbon sector in these countries was pushed into the politics of the budget.

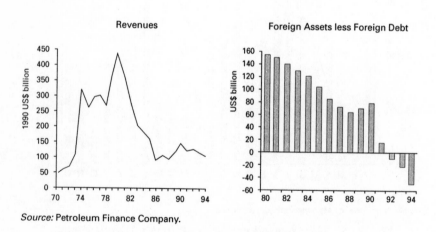

Source: Petroleum Finance Company.

Fig. 2.11   Real oil revenues and net assets of OPEC members

Very few oil-exporting countries still have the financial resources that they had a few years ago. Not only have their real oil revenues come down drastically in the past fifteen years, but also most countries have exhausted the vast financial surpluses accumulated during the 1970s and early 1980s and have instead had to accumulate debt. As Figure 2.11 shows, the net assets of OPEC member states (total foreign assets less total foreign debt), crashed from just under $160 billion in 1980 to almost *negative* $60 billion in 1994. But the depletion of assets and the accumulation of debt, in and of itself, is not a problem. The real problem facing these economies and these governments is the fact that money was not well spent – i.e., with no more than a few exceptions, none of the oil-exporting countries has managed to develop productive non-oil sectors that can grow and create wealth independently of government spending and subsidies. Thus, at a time when the hydrocarbon sectors are in dire need of investment, the political pressures on the governments to spend on either current or military items has, more often than not, deprived the oil and gas sectors of the necessary investment funds. This is why the budgets of the national oil companies, which in most countries do not represent important political constituencies, were the first to be cut.

Ironically, just when the demands on a declining revenue base started to take their toll on the governments' degrees of freedom in formulating domestic policy, their flexibility to influence oil markets virtually disappeared. The

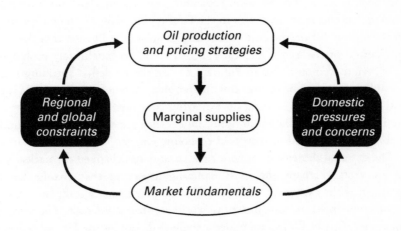

Fig. 2.12   The oil policy market fundamentals cycle

mounting domestic economic pressures meant that most governments could not afford the short-term revenue consequences of a campaign to raise their shrinking market share; nor could they afford to neglect a host of regional and global political repercussions while considering various short-term oil price targets.

Those oil-exporting countries in the Middle East that are politically independent of the West – Iran, Iraq, Libya – have been marginalized through sanctions. Those countries that depend on the West for their security (most GCC states) are generally constrained not only by the political imperative to spend on Western military and civilian imports, but also by the necessity to take Western economic interests into consideration while formulating oil policy. The former reduces their freedom to cut spending, the latter reduces their chances to raise oil revenues. Figure 2.12 depicts the constraints and implications of oil production and pricing policy through two important loops. Both start with the impact of a given production and pricing strategy on marginal supplies and, consequently, market fundamentals, but then branch out to the domestic and external implications of the market fundamentals, normally sending policy-makers back to the drawing board. In recent years, largely due to the general policy paralysis imposed by stricter domestic and external constraints, the "back to the drawing board" portions of the policy cycles have been seriously jeopardized.

The domestic constraints are intimately related to the fact that most oil-exporting governments of the Middle East have failed to come to terms with the new (post-oil boom) socio-economic realities in *their own* countries. Nowhere is this more true than in the Gulf region. Chronic deficit spending in the region during the past decade helped create the illusion that the carefree period of the 1970s and early 1980s could be indefinitely prolonged. However, as demonstrated in Figure 2.11, continued deficit spending is not a viable option for the future. But the problem cannot be reduced to a mere cost-cutting exercise. In most oil-exporting countries, cost-cutting measures are not viable, let alone meaningful, unless they are accompanied by fundamental structural and institutional economic reforms.

The external dimension of policy constraints has changed dramatically in recent years. Perhaps the most damning aspect of that change for oil exporters is the extremely stubborn and widespread supply complacency that has overwhelmed the oil-consuming world for almost a decade. The fact that three members of OPEC are under a trade embargo by the United States (a far cry from the supply anxiety days of the 1970s, when the main fear was that of oil-exporting countries boycotting the consumers) is indicative of the depth of supply complacency. The resilience of this complacency becomes even more remarkable when one considers the fact that it has survived major political and military upheavals, including two major wars in the Gulf, along with substantial reductions in excess production capacity in the world in the past few years.[5]

Part of the reason for the supply complacency is the substantial strategic petroleum reserves that were accumulated in most OECD countries after the first oil shock. Clearly, this provided a level of comfort for both governments and the industry. Another part is the hedging opportunities provided by the paper markets (discussed in more detail below). The very high consumer taxes are another reason for the supply complacency – a 30 percent increase in the price of crude oil translates into a mere 3 to 4 percent increase in the cost structure at the pump. Another part is the rapid increase in production capacity in countries outside of the Gulf, while the total capacity from the Gulf OPEC countries was on the decline. In fact, the cumulative additions to crude oil production capacity in the past fifteen years in just seven non-Gulf producing regions have far exceeded those of the Gulf OPEC members (see Figure 2.13).

Another interesting observation about Figure 2.13 is that in the selected non-Gulf producers group, all the capacity additions were undertaken by international oil companies, whereas in the Gulf group they were undertaken by national oil companies operating under governmental constraints. The

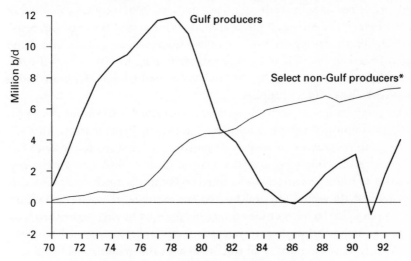

Note: * Norway, UK, Angola, Australia, Brunei/Malaysia and Alaska
Source: Petro Finance Upstream Competitor Service.

Fig. 2.13 Cumulative additions to capacity

clear message is that although oil remains largely a government-controlled business, governments and oil sectors do not necessarily mix well. This also demonstrates that the resource nationalism of the 1970s – which led many governments to nationalize their hydrocarbon sectors, driving the international majors out to invest in oil production capacity elsewhere – resulted in a considerable, albeit long-term, cost to those countries.

The Speculative Dimension

No discussion of a framework for understanding the global crude oil market would be complete without mentioning another important and relatively recent factor – namely, the proliferation of futures and forward markets and the nature of the various players in that area. The volume of trade in paper markets has increased substantially during the past decade and physical markets are by no means altogether immune from even short-term and highly speculative swings in paper market prices. Many physical traders have themselves become more sophisticated in the use of the various hedging and speculating opportunities provided by the paper markets. The result of this is the creation of an even closer relationship between the two markets.

The interaction between these two distinct but closely linked markets, paper and physical, has been one of the most significant forces shaping short-term trends not only in crude oil prices, but also in refinery behavior and in price differentials. Although physical markets are essentially regional, activity in any particular region is driven by the fundamentals of both global and regional markets, as well as by expectations formed by the perceived risks. Trade in paper is motivated by the need to buy and sell *risks* associated with the availability of future supplies.

The proliferation of risk management instruments contributed significantly to the supply complacency described earlier. Paper markets, through the hedging programs that they made possible, reduced the uncertainty factor considerably, simply because they were designed to deal with uncertainty. In case of a crunch, getting an order filled on Nymex is much easier than getting it filled through a physical broker. For example, the mere knowledge that it is possible to cover crude oil requirements by buying paper barrels on Nymex and then taking delivery makes a refiner less concerned with the declining level of one's crude oil stocks, or with the mounting political tension in a producing country or region. Thus, in addition to the transparency that paper markets have brought to the global crude oil marketplace, these markets have provided a tool for dealing with, and therefore reducing, the anxiety factor.

Paper markets are ultimately grounded in the fundamental realities of the physical market, but can, and periodically do, deviate from them. This is because futures prices reflect not only current fundamentals, but also perceptions of uncertainty about the future. These perceptions depend on a multitude of factors, including:

1. uncertainties regarding future economic growth, government policy and prospects for demand;
2. political factors that cause major shifts in marginal supplies;
3. technical trading factors which, in the absence of clear signals from the fundamentals, tend to dominate traders' decisions; and
4. motives and behavioral peculiarities of the main players.

The last point is central in shaping not only trends in paper markets, but also short-term perceptions. It is also one of the most difficult issues to monitor and quantify. However, even at the risk of oversimplifying matters somewhat, it is worth outlining the key characteristics of the main groups of players in paper markets. Five such groups will be briefly discussed in connection to their role in the paper crude oil markets.

Refiners

By the nature of their operations (buying crude oil and selling products), refiners are upside risk averse when it comes to crude oil prices. Since they are "natural shorts" in crude oil, any upward trend in crude oil prices, especially when not driven or accompanied by a rise in product prices, is of major concern to them. They tend to be buyers in rising markets, reinforcing the existing price trend.

Producers

Producers of crude oil are in the opposite position to refiners. They are downside risk averse and "natural longs" since they are in possession of crude oil for sale at all times, and tend to sell in falling markets – also helping reinforce an existing price trend.

Commodity funds

While refiners and producers are wet-barrel players that use paper markets, commodity funds may buy and sell paper barrels without ever having to handle physical crude oil. They are generally risk-seekers who, for whatever reasons, tend to buy paper oil to hold it as an investment, just as they would buy any other commodity. In that sense, they too are "natural longs" who tend to buy or at least hold on to their positions in a rising market. They are generally market followers and trade is largely driven by technical indicators.

Hedge funds

Hedge funds are also risk-seekers and display a much more speculative mode of trading in paper oil than do commodity funds. They are neither natural longs nor natural shorts, but use the paper oil market to either counterbalance or hedge some of their other portfolios. For example, a hedge fund with a position in bonds may get into the paper oil market with the calculation that any significant move in oil prices, through its impact on inflationary expectations, would have an opposite impact on bond prices. Thus, a hedge fund that is short in the bond market may buy large volumes of paper crude oil just to achieve desired results in the bond prices.

Financial firms

Financial firms are generally active on all fronts of financial instruments and they usually get into the paper oil market as arbitrageurs. Perhaps more than any other motive, they are driven by the need to offset some risk exposure from positions in other derivatives.

Conclusions

A relevant framework for understanding the commercial dynamics of the global crude oil market is one that meets the following criteria:

1. Focuses on commercially relevant geographic regions (rather than institutionally defined regions). The choice of regions, in turn, should be based on: a) crude oil quality, b) refinery complexity, c) structure of final demand, d) export patterns and tanker routes, e) production patterns and trends, and f) geographic and data considerations.

2. Is based on a commercially relevant time-structure that takes into account patterns of seasonality in crude oil and product markets and the timing of refinery turnarounds and crude oil maintenance shutdowns.

3. Acknowledges the fact that a very large proportion of the world's crude oil reserves is owned by governments and that decisions affecting investment in new capacity, as well as in production and exports, are still largely taken by governments. Moreover, recognizes the fact that the internal conditions in most producing countries have a profound influence over their external behavior, including oil policy.

4. Takes into account the significant and increasing influence that paper markets are having over physical markets, and tries to factor the speculative dimension into the analysis.

CHAPTER 3

Growing Energy Demand in Asian Countries: Opportunities and Constraints for Gulf Energy Exporters

Ken Koyama

As a result of rapid economic growth, energy demand in Asian developing countries is expected to experience very high growth rates in the foreseeable future. However, Asian countries will have limited domestic and regional energy supplies to meet this growth in their energy requirements. This is because of factors such as a limited resource base, high costs of new invest-ment in energy infrastructure, energy transportation bottlenecks, and grow-ing concern about environmental problems. These imbalances in energy demand and supply in Asian countries will bring out a heavier dependence on imported energy from outside the Asian region. This chapter will exam-ine the opportunities for Gulf energy exporters and the constraints which might inhibit Gulf penetration of the Asian market.

Growing Energy Demand in Asia

Trends in economic growth in Asia

Many Asian countries have achieved rapid economic growth in recent years. As shown in Table 3.1, gross national product (GNP) in 11 Asian countries' grew at an annual average rate of 4.9 percent from 1980 to 1992 in real terms. Above all, economic growth in Asian developing countries has been very high. The annual average growth rate of total GNP for 10 Asian devel-oping countries reached as high as 7.1 percent in the same period.

The rapid economic growth in Asian countries was brought about mainly by an increase in investment and exports (Koyama, 1992). First, many Asian countries experienced large increases in investment in the 1980s (Table 3.2). Asian developing countries were especially attractive to domestic and foreign capital investment because of the availability of cheap, educated, and

abundant labor. Large populations also implied potentially large future markets. An increase in investment can function as a multiplier. Furthermore, an
increase in investment can expand economic growth in the long term as it
raises the production capacity of an economy.

Table 3.1   Trends for economic growth in Asian countries

| | GNP in 1987 billion US$ | | | Average annual growth rate (%) | | |
	1980	1985	1992	85/80	92/85	92/80
Japan	1,877	2,262	2,988	3.8	4.1	4.0
ROK	68	101	192	8.4	9.5	9.1
Taiwan	65	91	159	7.1	8.2	7.8
China	177	286	491	10.1	8.1	8.9
Hong Kong	28	37	59	5.6	7.0	6.4
Singapore	13	19	30	7.7	7.0	7.3
Indonesia	50	65	101	5.4	6.5	6.0
Malaysia	22	27	46	4.2	7.7	6.3
Thailand	32	42	78	5.4	9.4	7.7
Philippines	33	30	39	−1.8	3.9	1.5
India	181	232	330	5.1	5.1	5.1
Total	2,545	3,192	4,513	4.6	5.1	4.9
(excl. Japan)	668	930	1,525	6.8	7.3	7.1

Source: World Bank, 1994.

Table 3.2   Growth in investments and exports in Asian countries

	Growth in investment (%) 1980–93	Growth in exports (%) 1980–92
Japan	5.5	4.2
ROK	11.8	12.8
China	11.1	11.0
Singapore	5.7	8.6
Indonesia	7.1	2.8
Malaysia	6.3	10.3
Thailand	11.4	13.2
Philippines	−0.1	2.5
India	5.7	6.5
(World average)	3.2	4.3

Source: World Bank, 1995.

Second, a rapid increase in exports supported economic growth in Asian
countries. Exports increased substantially in the 1980s (Table 3.2) as world
economic growth, especially in the US in the second half of the 1980s,
absorbed the Asian exports. In addition, exports (and imports) among Asian
countries expanded as domestic demand in those countries grew, accelerated

by the increased level of income. Thus, in many Asian countries, increase in investments, exports, and income level formed a favorable environment for economic growth.

Consequently, important factors determining economic growth in Asia in the future are likely to be investment trends in Asia, economic growth in the US and other industrialized countries, and world economic trends. It is also important to note economic strains emerging recently in some Asian countries caused by excessively rapid economic growth. Economic strains such as inflation caused by the overheating of an economy, inequality in income distribution, and bottlenecks caused by insufficient infrastructure might restrain Asian economic growth in the future. Judging from currently available information, however, it is quite likely that most Asian countries can maintain high economic growth, backed by active investments, expanding domestic consumption, and increase in intra/inter-regional trade.

Relation between economic growth and energy demand

Increase in economic activity and income brought about by economic growth can expand energy demand in various ways. In the industrial sector, increased levels of production require an increase in the use of energy as an input factor. In the household sector, income growth can bring about increased demand for energy appliances and shifts toward more energy dependent lifestyles. In addition, income growth in developing countries can often promote shifts in fuel use from traditional energy like fuel woods, charcoal, and animal residue, to commercial energy like oil (kerosene, LPG), natural gas, and coal. Thus energy demand in the household sector can increase with economic growth. In the transportation sector, energy demand grows as income growth brings about an increase in the number and the uses of vehicles. Energy demand also grows as increased economic activity and growth in transportation infrastructure raise transportation demands of passengers and goods.

Figure 3.1 shows the relation between income per capita and energy consumption per capita in Asian countries. It can be seen that energy consumption has increased with economic growth (increased income) in each country. Comparison by country also indicates in general that if a country's income level is higher than another, so is its energy consumption level. Considering differences in economic structure and energy demand structure in each country, it should be a matter of course that each country will experience different growth rates for both economy and energy demand in the future. However, it is also likely that Asian developing countries will experience bigger energy demand with economic growth, following the industrialized countries not only in terms of economic development but also in terms of energy demand.

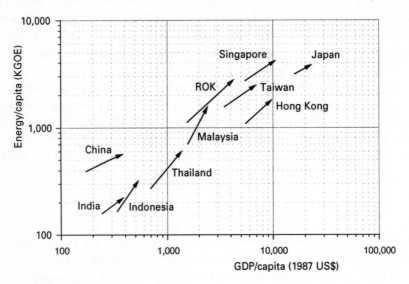

Source: IEA; World Bank.

Fig. 3.1   Changes in GDP/capita and energy consumption/capita by country, 1980–92

Trends for energy demand growth in Asia

Backed by rapid economic growth, total primary energy demand in 11 Asian countries increased from 1.03 billion tonnes oil equivalent (TOE) in 1980 to 1.72 billion TOE in 1992 at an annual average rate of 4.4 percent (Table 3.3). Energy demand growth in Asian developing countries was especially high. The growth rate of total energy demand excluding Japan reached 5.5 percent in the same period. Furthermore, it is indicated that energy demand growth in Asian countries accelerated in the latter half of the 1980s, along with the accelerated economic growth.

In 1992, China had the largest primary energy demand in Asia (710 million TOE), followed by Japan (467 million TOE), India (206 million TOE), Republic of Korea (ROK) (114 million TOE), Indonesia (59 million TOE), and Taiwan (54 million TOE). On the other hand, the annual average growth rate of energy demand in Malaysia was the highest among Asian countries at 9.5 percent from 1980 to 1992, followed by Thailand (9.3 percent), and ROK (8.8 percent). The growth rates for other

Asian developing countries were also high at around 6.7 percent in the same period. By contrast, Japan's energy demand growth was much lower than that of neighboring countries, staying as low as 2.0 percent in the same period.

Table 3.3   Trends for energy demand growth in Asian countries

	Primary energy demand (MTOE)			Average annual growth rate (%)		
	1980	1985	1992	85/80	92/85	92/80
Japan	369	378	467	0.5	3.1	2.0
ROK	41	54	114	5.3	11.4	8.8
Taiwan	28	33	54	3.5	7.3	5.7
China	412	540	710	5.6	4.0	4.6
Hong Kong	6	7	11	6.0	5.4	5.7
Singapore	6	8	13	5.9	7.2	6.7
Indonesia	25	32	59	4.7	9.2	7.3
Malaysia	9	13	28	7.0	11.4	9.5
Thailand	12	16	36	5.8	11.9	9.3
Philippines	13	12	20	−2.1	7.7	3.5
India	105	137	206	5.5	6.0	5.8
Total	1,026	1,230	1,716	3.7	4.9	4.4
(excl. Japan)	658	852	1,249	5.3	5.6	5.5

Source: IEA, 1994a, 1994b.

Table 3.4   Outlook for economic growth in Asian countries

	GNP in 1987 billion US$			Average annual growth rate		
	1992	2000	2010	00/92	10/00	10/92
Japan	2,988	3,785	4,845	3.0	2.5	2.7
ROK	192	329	536	7.0	5.0	5.9
Taiwan	159	254	413	6.0	5.0	5.4
China	491	978	1,925	9.0	7.0	7.9
Hong Kong	59	95	154	6.0	5.0	5.4
Singapore	30	48	79	6.0	5.1	5.5
Indonesia	101	167	292	6.5	5.7	6.1
Malaysia	46	76	134	6.5	5.7	6.1
Thailand	78	133	238	6.9	6.0	6.4
Philippines	39	58	94	5.0	5.0	5.0
India	330	506	906	5.5	6.0	5.8
Total	4,513	6,429	9,616	4.5	4.1	4.3
(excl. Japan)	1,525	2,644	4,772	7.1	6.1	6.5

Source: Koyama, 1995.

Outlook for economic growth and energy demand in Asia

Table 3.4 illustrates the outlook for economic growth in Asian countries given by the author. Total GNP in 11 Asian countries increased at an annual average rate of 4.9 percent from 1980 to 1992 and is expected to keep growing at 4.5 percent from 1992 to 2000 and at 4.1 percent from 2000 to 2010. Among Asian countries, China is expected to experience the highest economic growth at 9 percent from 1992 to 2000 and at 7 percent from 2000 to 2010. Economic growth rate for other Asian developing countries is also expected to be very high at around 6–7 percent (1992–2000) and at around 5–6 percent (2000–2010). On the other hand, economic growth in Japan is expected to remain low compared to Asian developing countries, at around 2 percent from now on. This view seems to be modest (for example, see Matsui, 1994 and Fujime, 1995), as the author takes account of the possible bottleneck for future economic growth, which was mentioned previously, more seriously.

As a result of expected economic growth, energy demand in Asia will also increase rapidly. Total primary energy demand in 11 Asian countries is expected to increase from 1.72 billion TOE in 1992 to 2.42 billion TOE in 2000 and 3.48 billion TOE in 2010 at an annual average growth rate of 4.4 percent (1992–2000) and at 3.7 percent (2000–2010). Energy demand in Asian developing countries will keep growing at a higher rate. It is expected that the growth rate of energy demand in 10 Asian developing countries will increase at 5.3 percent (1992–2000) and at 4.3 percent (2000–2010). Table 3.5 shows expected energy demand growth in Asia from 1992 to 2010 by country. China, India, and ROK are expected to lead energy demand growth in terms of incremental volume but Indonesia, Malaysia, and Thailand are expected to lead in terms of growth rate.

Table 3.5   Outlook for primary energy demand in Asian countries

| | Primary energy demand (MTOE) | | | Average annual growth rate | | | Increment |
	1992	2000	2010	00/92	10/00	10/92	10–92
Japan	467	539	610	1.8	1.2	1.5	143
ROK	114	186	288	6.3	4.5	5.3	174
Taiwan	54	75	105	4.2	3.5	3.8	52
China	710	1,009	1,386	4.5	3.2	3.8	676
Hong Kong	11	19	27	7.2	3.6	5.2	16
Singapore	13	19	29	5.4	4.1	4.7	16
Indonesia	59	109	197	8.1	6.0	6.9	138
Malaysia	28	50	89	7.6	5.8	6.6	61
Thailand	36	65	118	7.9	6.1	6.9	83
Philippines	20	33	61	6.4	6.3	6.3	41
India	206	316	565	5.5	6.0	5.8	360
Total	1,716	2,421	3,476	4.4	3.7	4.0	1,760
(excl. Japan)	1,249	1,882	2,866	5.3	4.3	4.7	1,617

Source: Koyama, 1995.

Constraints on Increases in Energy Production

Resource base constraints

Oil: Proven oil reserves in Asia stood at 42.8 billion barrels' at the end of 1994 (BP, 1995). The reserve per production (R/P) ratio for oil in Asia was 18.1, based on oil production of 6.48 million barrels per day (b/d) in 1994. Furthermore, the same amount of oil production in Asia could meet only 40 percent of oil demand in Asia (Table 3.6).

Table 3.6   Reserves, production, and R/P for each fossil fuel in Asia at the end of 1994

	Oil	Coal	Natural gas
Reserves	42.8	220.4	328.1
	(bil. barrel)	(bil. ton)	(tril. cf)
Production	6,480	787.5	154.4
	(1,000b/d)	(MTOE)	(MTOE)
R/P	18.1	136.6	54.2
Consumption	15,975	878.4	163.3
	(1,000b/d)	(MTOE)	(MTOE)

Source: BP, 1995.

   Although the R/P ratio was 18.1, it does not imply that oil will run out in Asia in 18.1 years. The R/P ratio is a result of a simple calculation in which proved reserves are divided by current production. Consequently, the R/P ratio varies according to changes in production level and proven reserves, both of which vary. Proven reserves, in particular, defined as recoverable volume under existing economic and operational conditions,[3] can even increase without the discovery of new reservoirs. They can increase with the use of new technology or new methods of cost reduction.

   Nevertheless, oil resources in Asia alone are unlikely to meet growing oil demand in Asia, given that current oil production falls short of current oil demand and that oil demand is expected to increase rapidly.

Coal: Proven coal reserves in Asia stood at 220.4 billion tonnes at the end of 1994. Total coal production in Asia (787.5 million TOE) in 1994 accounted for around 90 percent of total coal consumption in Asia (878.4 million TOE). Based on production in 1994, the R/P ratio for coal can be calculated at as high as 136.6. In this sense, coal resources in Asia are ample compared to oil resources.

Natural gas: Proven natural gas reserves in Asia stood at 328.1 trillion cubic feet at the end of 1994. Total natural gas production in Asia (154.4 million TOE) was almost equal to total natural gas consumption in Asia (163.3 million TOE). Based on production in 1994, the R/P ratio for natural gas can be calculated at 54.3. Natural gas in Asia is close to coal in terms of regional demand and supply balances but is close to oil in terms of the R/P ratio.

From the above observations, it can be argued that in Asia coal resources are the most ample and oil resources are the most scarce.[4]

Energy infrastructure constraints

Energy resources in the form of reserves are not usable as energy directly. They have to be developed, produced, transformed into usable energy, and transported to consumers. Various infrastructures are required for energy production, transformation, and transportation. Examples of these are development and production facilities in coal mines and oil/gas fields, oil refineries, natural gas liquefaction facilities, power stations, oil/gas pipelines, oil and LNG tankers, power transmission/distribution lines, railroads, roads, and harbor facilities.

In this way, a number of infrastructures are involved in an energy supply network, and a problem in one energy infrastructure might result in a bottleneck in another. Problems have emerged recently which have caused investment in energy infrastructures in Asia to be delayed or to stagnate (Kanayama, 1995; Morita, 1995; Koyama, 1995; Ogawa, 1995; Toichi, 1994). Delays and stagnation in investment are caused mainly by concern for the economics of the investment or by environmental problems.

In general, investment in energy infrastructure tends to be large, because of the economy of scale for the energy infrastructure. It also tends to have a long pay-back period and a long lead time for construction and operation. An investor, especially a foreign investor who requires hard currency returns from the investment, is apt to be cautious about investment in energy infrastructures, given these characteristics. In these circumstances, the economics of investment for some energy infrastructures have deteriorated recently because of higher costs for investment and lower energy prices. Typical examples can be observed in the case of the new grass-roots refinery and LNG projects (Koyama, 1995; Ogawa, 1995; Toichi, 1994). Investments in these projects require large amounts of money and their economics have deteriorated, as required investment costs have risen for various reasons, and refinery margins and crude oil prices have stayed at low levels. Another factor to be considered is the political and economic risk in a country in which the investment might be made (Koyama, 1995; Ogawa, 1995). Hence, investment for many of these new grass-roots projects has recently stagnated.

Investment for an energy project to develop domestic resources for domestic use faces other economic problems, specifically financial constraints. Considering that this kind of project can be less attractive to a foreign investor because of possible constraints on convertibility of currency and earning remittance, and that domestic capital in developing countries is often not available, financial constraints can pose a serious problem for the project. An example of this case is a bottleneck of railroad transportation capacity for coal supply in China (Kanayama, 1995; Morita, 1995).

Environmental problems can affect construction of energy infrastructures in three ways. First, construction of an energy facility in which large amounts of fuel are consumed may be seen as contributing to air pollution and global warming. In this context, the construction of coal-fired power stations in particular may be restricted in order to limit coal consumption. Second, construction and operation of an energy infrastructure is restricted because it is regarded as a direct threat to the environment at, and around, the site of the infrastructure. For example, construction of large-scale hydro-power stations can be curbed for this reason. Potentially, however, such concern can apply to all energy infrastructure construction. Third, construction of an energy infrastructure is restricted by the concern about serious and widespread damage in case of an accident. The most typical example of this case is limiting the construction of nuclear power stations.

Each Asian country accords different priorities to different environmental problems. For example, the issue of global warming has become an important energy policy consideration in Japan (MITI, 1990), but it has often been given lower priority than urban air pollution in other developing countries (Itabashi and Ichino, 1994). In almost all the countries, however, environmental problems are expected to influence choice of energy supply source and energy supply capacity in the future. In particular, the supply capacity of coal and nuclear power is subject to environmental concern.

To sum up, it is expected that an increase in energy production in Asian countries may be restricted in the future by the various factors mentioned above and will not be able to match rapidly growing energy demand. It is expected that the future crucial constraints on energy production in Asian countries will be resource-based constraints involving oil, constraints associated with the economics of energy infrastructures for natural gas (LNG) and coal, and constraints arising from environmental problems for coal and nuclear.

Opportunities for Gulf Penetration

Asian energy imports from outside the region are expected to increase substantially, with rapid energy demand growth and restricted energy production within the region. The expected widening imbalances between energy demand and production in Asia can provide opportunities for all energy exporters outside the region, including Gulf energy exporters. This section examines the outlook for supply and demand of oil and natural gas (LNG) in Asia to analyze the potential for Gulf exports to penetrate the markets.

Table 3.7   Outlook for oil demand in Asian countries

	Oil demand (million b/d)				Average annual growth rate (%)		
	1985	1993	2000	2005	93/85	00/85	05/00
Japan	4.4	5.5	5.9	6.1	2.8	1.0	0.7
ROK	0.5	1.6	2.2	2.7	15.2	5.2	4.3
Taiwan	0.4	0.6	0.7	0.8	5.2	3.0	3.0
China	1.9	3.0	4.2	5.1	6.1	5.0	4.0
Singapore	0.2	0.5	0.6	0.7	8.8	4.4	1.8
Indonesia	0.4	0.8	1.2	1.6	8.0	6.4	5.9
Malaysia	0.2	0.3	0.4	0.5	8.6	5.2	4.7
Thailand	0.2	0.5	0.8	1.1	11.3	7.2	5.5
Philippines	0.2	0.3	0.4	0.5	2.4	5.5	4.9
India	0.8	1.3	1.9	2.3	6.0	5.9	4.3
Others	0.8	1.1	1.6	2.0	4.8	5.3	4.6
Total	10.0	15.3	20.0	23.5	5.5	3.9	3.3
(excl. Japan)	5.6	9.8	14.1	17.4	7.2	5.3	4.3

Source: Koyama, 1995; Toichi and Kashio, 1994.

Outlook for oil imports

Backed by strong economic growth, oil demand in Asia[5] increased from 10.0 million b/d in 1985 to 15.3 million b/d in 1993 (Table 3.7). Oil demand in Asia, especially in developing countries, is expected to keep growing, supported by an increase in such factors as the number of passenger cars, buses and trucks, transportation demand for goods and passengers, capacity of ethylene crackers which uses naphtha as a feedstock, and fuel demand for industry and power generation (Koyama, 1995; Toichi and Kashio, 1994, Wu, 1995). According to projections by the Institute of Energy Economics (IEE), Japan, oil demand in Asia is expected to increase to 20.0 million b/d in 2000 and to 23.5 million b/d in 2005.

By country, oil demand growth rates in ROK, China, Indonesia, Malaysia, Thailand, and India are expected to be high at around 5–6 percent (1992–2000) and 4–5 percent (2000–2010). By contrast, oil demand in Japan is expected to grow at a little less than 1 percent from now on. In terms of incremental volume of oil demand, China, ROK, and India are expected to experience large gains. The increase in oil demand of the three countries combined is expected to reach 4.2 million b/d from 1993 to 2005.

Table 3.8   Outlook for oil production in Asian countries

| | Oil production (million b/d) | | | |
	1985	1993	2000	2005
China	2.5	2.9	3.2	3.3
Indonesia	1.3	1.5	1.3	1.2
Malaysia	0.4	0.6	0.7	0.6
India	0.6	0.6	0.7	0.7
Brunei	0.2	0.2	0.2	0.2
Vietnam	0.0	0.1	0.3	0.4
PNG	0.0	0.1	0.1	0.1
Others	0.1	0.1	0.1	0.1
Total	5.1	6.2	6.6	6.6

Source: Koyama, 1993, 1995.

On the other hand, oil production in Asia totaled 6.2 million b/d in 1993 (Table 3.8). The main oil producers in Asia are China, Indonesia, India, and Malaysia. Vietnam and Papua New Guinea recently became new oil producers. Many oil-producing countries in Asia have actively introduced capital and technology from foreign oil companies into their upstream sectors. Following this trend, some producing countries are expecting their oil production to increase in the future. Nevertheless, oil production in Asia cannot be expected to increase substantially as a whole, because production in many Asian countries is expected to be leveled off and to decrease in the long run (Koyama, 1993, 1995; Wu, 1995).

An examination of situations of current oil production and trends for oil exploration and development by country shows that oil production in China and Vietnam is expected to increase from 2.9 million b/d in 1993 to 3.3 million b/d in 2005 and from 0.13 million b/d in 1993 to 0.4 million b/d in 2005, respectively. It is also expected that oil production in Malaysia and Brunei will be leveled off and that oil production in Indonesia will gradually decline in the long run. As a result, oil production in Asia as a whole is expected to increase a little from the current level and to stay at 6.6 million b/d from 2000 to 2005.

Table 3.9   Outlook for net oil imports in Asian countries

	Net oil imports (million b/d)				Increment (million b/d)		
	1985	1993	2000	2005	93/85	00/93	05/00
Japan	4.1	5.3	5.6	5.8	1.2	0.3	0.2
ROK	0.5	1.6	2.1	2.6	1.1	0.6	0.5
Taiwan	0.4	0.6	0.7	0.8	0.2	0.1	0.1
China	−0.6	0.1	1.0	1.8	0.7	0.9	0.8
Singapore	0.2	0.5	0.6	0.7	0.2	0.2	0.1
Indonesia	−0.9	−0.8	−0.1	0.4	0.1	0.6	0.5
Malaysia	−0.3	−0.4	−0.3	−0.1	−0.1	0.1	0.2
Thailand	0.2	0.5	0.8	1.0	0.3	0.3	0.3
Philippines	0.2	0.2	0.3	0.4	0.0	0.1	0.1
India	0.2	0.7	1.2	1.6	0.5	0.5	0.4
Others	0.5	0.6	0.9	1.3	0.1	0.3	0.3
Total	4.5	8.9	12.9	16.3	4.4	4.0	3.4

Source: Koyama, 1993, 1995; Toichi and Kashio, 1994.

Asian oil imports will increase, with rapid growth in oil demand and a limited increase in oil production (Table 3.9). In Asia, net oil import, defined as oil demand minus oil production, is expected to increase from 8.9 million b/d in 1993 to 12.9 million b/d in 2000 and to 16.3 million b/d in 2005 (Koyama, 1993, 1995; Toichi and Kashio, 1994). China, ROK, India, and Thailand are expected to experience large increases in net oil imports. China, becoming a net oil importer in 1993, is expected to require net oil imports of around 2 million b/d in 2005. Indonesia, the largest oil exporter in Asia currently, is expected to lose its oil export availability swiftly and to become a net oil importer of 0.4 million b/d in 2005.

Outlook for natural gas (LNG) imports

Natural gas can be exported from a gas-producing country to a consuming country either by pipeline or in the form of liquefied natural gas (LNG). In the Asian market, natural gas has mainly been traded in the form of LNG. This is because the gas-importing countries, Japan, ROK, and Taiwan, are far away by sea from gas-producing countries. Thus, a knowledge of the outlook for LNG demand and supply in Asia is essential for assessing opportunities for Gulf gas producers in the future.

LNG demand in Asia is expected to increase rapidly, as natural gas becomes more popular as a clean fuel, and efficient gas combined cycle power generation becomes popular (Morita, 1993, 1995; Toichi, 1994). Asian LNG demand totaled 46.9 million tonnes in 1993, of which Japan accounted for 40.0 million tonnes, ROK for 4.4 million tonnes, and Taiwan for 2.6 million tonnes (Table 3.10). According to IEE's view, LNG demand in each of these three Asian countries will experience a substantial increase and total LNG demand is expected to reach 70–73 million tonnes in 2000 and 93–95 million tonnes in 2010.

Table 3.10 LNG demand and supply outlook for Japan, ROK, and Taiwan (million tonnes/year)

Demand	1993	2000	2010
Japan	40.0	53–54	58–60
ROK	4.4	10	20
Taiwan	2.6	7	15
Total	46.9	70–73	93–95
Secured supply	1993	2000	2010
Japan		52	48–52
ROK		6	5–6
Taiwan		4	4
Total		62	57–62
Balance (required additional supply)	1993	2000	2010
	–	8–11	31–38
Import source of secured supply	1993	2000	2010
Asia	38	44	40–44
Non-Asia	8.9	18	18

Source: Morita, 1993, 1995; Toichi, 1994.

In addition, LNG import projects have recently been planned in China, India, and Thailand (Morita, 1995). So far, those projects have not been confirmed, and whether they will be realized or not remains uncertain. But if they are realized, LNG demand in Asia will be greater than that predicted above by the IEE.

LNG transactions are normally based on a long-term contract in which a contracted volume of LNG is to be supplied to the consumer. Thus, in examining future LNG demand and supply balances, it is essential to first check how much LNG demand in the future is secured by current contract. An investigation into LNG demand in Japan, ROK, and Taiwan indicates that secured LNG supply by current contract from existing LNG projects and confirmed LNG projects is expected to total 62 million tonnes in 2000 and 57–62 million tonnes in 2010 (Morita, 1995; Toichi, 1994).

Therefore, the difference between LNG demand and secured supply by current contract has to be met by supply from either expansion of production capacity in existing projects, or new grass-roots projects. This is expected to reach 8–11 million tonnes in 2000 and 31–38 million tonnes in 2010.

Existing projects alone are expected to expand LNG production by more than 10 million tonnes (Toichi, 1994), but supply from new grass-roots projects will be essential in the longer term. There are a number of planned new grass-roots LNG projects[6] both in, and outside of, Asia, as shown in Table 3.11.

Table 3.11   New grass-roots LNG (natural gas) projects for Asian market

Project	Production capacity (million tonnes/year)	Project partner
Indonesia (Natuna)	14	Pertamina/Exxon
Malaysia (MLNG-3)	5	Petronas/Occidental/Nippon oil
PNG (Pandora)	5	Mobil/IPC/SK/Nippon oil/others
PNG (Hides)	6	BP/Chebron/Mitsubishi oil/others
Qatar (Qatar gas)	4	QGPC/Mobil/Total/Mitsui Corp./Mitsubishi Corp.
Qatar (Ras Laffan LNG)	10	QGPC/Mobil
Qatar (Elf/Sumitomo)	4	QGPC/Elf/Sumitomo Corp.
Oman	5	Oman government/Shell/Total/Others
Yemen	5	Exxon/Hunt/Yukong, Enron
Alaska	14	Arco/Exxon/BP/others
Australia (Bonaparte)	2	Santos/Osaka gas/Sumitomo Corp./Teikoku oil
Australia (Gorgon)	6	Shell/Chebron/Texaco/Ampolex
Russia (Sakhalin 1)	6	Sodeco/Exxon
Russia (Sakhalin 2)	6	Marathon/McDermot/Mitsui Corp./others
Turkmenistan	10–15	CNPC/Mitsubishi Corp.
Yakutsk	15	Siberia Natural Gas

Source: Toichi, 1994.

LNG supply in the Asian market in 1993 can be broken down into supply from within Asia (38 million tonnes) and that from outside of Asia (9 million tonnes). An examination of LNG supply in the future indicates that secured supply by contract from within Asia is expected to increase to 44 million tonnes in 2000 and 40–44 million tonnes in 2010. Secured supply, however, from outside Asia is expected to grow faster, doubling from the 1993 level to 18 million tonnes in 2000 and 2010. Furthermore, most of the new grass-roots LNG projects are being planned outside Asia. Thus it is possible to expect that Asian countries, anticipating widening LNG demand and supply imbalances, will increase LNG imports from outside the region, including imports from Gulf gas exporters.

Constraints on Gulf Penetration of the Asian Oil and Gas Market

The previous part of the chapter examined the energy demand and supply situation in Asia and pointed out that the expected widening gap between demand and supply of oil and LNG in Asia could provide opportunities for Gulf energy exports to penetrate the Asian market.

However, these are only opportunities, and it is still uncertain whether or not Gulf penetration of the Asian oil and gas markets can be realized as expected. Faced with the outlook that Gulf exports of oil and LNG to the Asian market will increase sharply, Asian governments and industries might adopt and implement policies to restrict Gulf penetration of their market. This could be achieved by using the following strategies. Demand could be reduced by means of conservation and fuel substitution; oil and gas (LNG) production could be increased in Asia; the oil and gas (LNG) import source could be diversified;[7] investment by Gulf oil and gas producers in their domestic market could be regulated. These policies and strategies could be implemented by such approaches as command (e.g., a statutory obligation for energy conservation), persuasion (e.g., a TV campaign for energy conservation), and market (e.g., tax on energy) (Stevens, 1995a).

The policies and strategies mentioned above are motivated by concern for the security of supply and by the concern of existing players in the Asian energy market that they might lose their market to Gulf oil and gas penetration.

Concern for security of supply

The relation between energy import dependence – especially import dependence on Middle East oil – and energy security has been widely discussed. On the one hand, it has been argued that there is no direct link between energy import dependence and energy security (Lichtblau, 1994; Niskanen, 1988). On the other hand, however, arguments that increased dependence on imported energy, especially oil from the Middle East, is a threat to energy security (API, 1985, 1988; DOC, 1988, 1994; Hogan, 1987) have provided a driving force for energy policies and strategies in the past.

Increased dependence on imported oil from the Middle East can impair the importing country's energy security, on the ground that oil supply disruption causes serious adverse effects on the national economy of the importing country and that there is concern for supply disruption particularly in the case of oil imports from the Middle East.

Physical shortages of oil and higher prices of oil, both of which can be brought about by oil supply disruption, cause serious damage to the economy of an oil-importing country. They can reduce output and operation in the industry sector, and can bring about loss of GNP and unemployment. Physical shortages of gasoline and electricity, in turn, reduce energy supply to consumers and affect civil/economic life negatively. Additionally, higher oil prices, often increasing the amount of import payments, make the importing country's balance of payments worse. Higher oil prices, increasing energy input costs causing upward pressures on general prices, can raise inflation in the importing country, even though higher oil prices can affect a country not dependent on oil imports in the same way.

Political instability in the Middle East has been identified as a possible future cause of disruption of supplies (API, 1985; DOC, 1988). Those who have pointed out the instability of the Middle East often state that Middle East countries suffer from political and social friction within their countries, and between countries, some of which have actually caused wars and revolution in the past. In addition to the instability in the Middle East itself, confrontation between the US and the Soviet Union in the Cold War period built up tensions which amplified that instability.

Nowadays, however, the ability of oil-importing countries to mitigate the adverse effects of oil supply disruption has improved by means of building up (government) oil stockpiles (Lichtblau, 1994; Mitchell, 1994), diversification of energy supply sources, and increased capacities for fuel switching. Oil supply disruption in the Middle East is now regarded as less likely than in the past, on the grounds that the Cold War is over and that the Middle East oil exporters, suffering from reduced oil revenues caused by significant declines in oil prices since 1986, have recognized reciprocal economic relations between oil-importing countries and oil-exporting countries (Fried and Trezise, 1993; Lichtblau, 1994; Mitchell, 1994).

In this context, concern for security of supply regarding oil imports from the Middle East has diminished in oil-importing countries in general, and in Asian countries in particular. Lower oil prices have nevertheless affected the economics of new investment for energy conservation and alternative energy development negatively. Furthermore, because Asian countries are now faced with growing requirements to meet their rapidly increasing energy demands, the lower cost of oil has not provided the necessary incentive for these oil-importing countries to reduce their oil imports from the Middle East. (Lichtblau, 1994).

However, this does not necessarily mean that concern for security supply is no longer important. Oil supply disruption can still cause serious damage to the economy of an oil-importing country, even though the ability of the country to mitigate the damage might have improved. Oil supply disruption might be less likely now than in the past, but it cannot be ruled out in the future. Concern for security of supply has decreased but remains in governments and industries in oil-importing countries, including Asian countries. If dependence on imported oil increases as expected in Asian countries, concern for security of supply may surface again, especially in times of Middle East unrest.

Concern of existing players in the Asian energy market that they might lose their market through Gulf penetration

Gulf penetration of oil and gas markets in Asia can conflict with the interests of existing players who are trying to maintain or expand their market. These players might try to restrict Gulf penetration of their market to protect their own interests. The government of an importing country might try to restrict Gulf penetration as well, to protect existing players in the country regarded as important to the nation's economy.

The extent of existing players' concern varies, depending on the impacts made by Gulf penetration of their particular market. The impact can be different in each of the oil, gas, and other energy markets and the effect on exporters and on importers can also be different.

The impact on the oil and gas market will be examined first. For Asian exporters of oil and gas, Gulf penetration of their markets can pose serious problems. This is because Asian exporters and Gulf exporters are competing for the same market and increased oil and gas exports from the Gulf might directly reduce the Asian exporters' share. Gulf penetration might be more serious in the gas market, where Asian gas-producing countries have many plans, including plans for grass-roots projects, to increase their production and exports of LNG.

However, Gulf penetration of the oil market might be unimportant to Asian oil exporters, because Asian exporters will soon lose their export availability due to growing domestic demand, with some exporters actually becoming net oil importers. Moreover, markets for Gulf crude and Asian crude can be different due to the differences in quality, for example in sulfur content, pour point and specific gravity.

Importers in the oil and gas market in Asia are basically customers of Gulf exporters. As long as mere relations between exporters and their customers remain unchanged, Gulf penetration matters little to importers. However, Gulf penetration of the downstream market might pose a threat to importers, changing the competitive situation in the market.

Thus, Gulf penetration matters little to gas importers in Asia, as Asian downstream gas markets are regulated markets and in many cases monopolized markets where new entry by the Gulf is unlikely in the foreseeable future.[8] In the Asian downstream oil market, however, importers such as local oil companies, national oil companies, and majors are competing with each other for the market. Gulf penetration of this market would mean that existing players would lose some of their market share.

Even in other energy markets, Gulf penetration can be a problem to players if their interests compete with oil and gas. For example, it is expected that electricity demand in many of the Asian countries will increase very rapidly (Matsuo and Higashida, 1995) and that both oil and gas, but gas especially, will compete with other energy sources for a market share in the growing fuel market for power generation. Consequently, Gulf penetration, through inter-fuel competition, can take the market from producers and exporters of energy other than oil and gas.[9]

In the current circumstances of economic liberalization and deregulation it is difficult for existing players and governments concerned with Gulf penetration to argue for the protection of their market share and interests or protection of their domestic industry straightforwardly. Instead, their arguments regarding Gulf penetration might be justified by concern for security of supply.

As mentioned earlier, concern for security of supply nowadays is less intense. But if such concern emerges again with the tightening of the oil and gas market, the influence of existing players and governments who are concerned about Gulf penetration for their own reasons may be intensified as well.

Current situations for regulation/deregulation of energy markets in Asia

Governments in Asian countries have so far not implemented statutory restrictions on oil and gas imports from Gulf countries or on investments by Gulf energy exporters in their domestic downstream markets. Nevertheless, broad policies and strategies for energy security aimed at reducing oil import dependency and diversification of energy supply source have been adopted and implemented. These strategies have resulted in restricting Gulf penetration and making access to the downstream market in Asia difficult for the Gulf.[10]

Under existing circumstances, it is unlikely that governments in Asian countries would adopt policies and strategies to directly regulate and restrict Gulf penetration of the energy market in their countries. Furthermore, from an economic standpoint, it is now difficult for governments in many Asian countries to intensify intervention in their energy market aimed at restraining oil and gas demand and diversification of energy supplies. This is because costs of intervention have become higher as lower prices of oil in the world market since 1986 affected the economics of investment for energy conservation and alternative energy development. In this context, an increase in oil and gas imports in Asian countries from the Gulf in the future is considered a "natural" result, taking into account trends for energy demand and pro-

duction balances in Asia and oil and gas resources and production capacity in
the Gulf.

Moreover, economic liberalization and deregulation is becoming increasingly popular in the world. As a result, the energy market is moving in
the same direction as worldwide market liberalization, deregulation, and
less government intervention in general. In Asia, much progress on market liberalization and deregulation has been made recently in downstream
oil markets.

In Japan, the liberalization of oil product imports will be developed, by
abolishing the law regulating oil imports. This was scheduled to be (and
actually was) completed at the end of March 1996 (Koide, 1995). In ROK,
oil product pricing has been gradually liberalized since 1983 (Fuji, 1995) and
in Taiwan new entry has been allowed to the downstream market monopolized by the Chinese Petroleum Corporation (Koide, 1994). In China, oil
market reforms and liberalization have developed in a "stop-and-go" way
(Ogawa, 1995) and in India, there has been a partial liberalization on oil
product imports and pricing (IEE, 1994). Still, there are many projects
planned in Asian countries to construct new refineries by introduction of foreign capital¹¹ (Koyama, 1995) and Gulf investments have already been made
in the Asian downstream oil market, for example by Saudi Arabia in ROK
and the Philippines, and by Kuwait in Thailand. Saudi Arabia and Kuwait
are also planning further investments in Asian countries (Toichi, Yamazaki
and Horie, 1995).

These trends for deregulation and liberalization in the market will not
necessarily provide a driving force to promote Gulf penetration straightforwardly. But progress in deregulation and liberalization in the energy market, in general, can at least prevent an unfavorable environment for Gulf
penetration in that deregulation and liberalization result in less intervention
by the government.

Trends for liberalization and deregulation, however, can take a different
direction according to changes in surrounding situations for the world
and/or one country's economy and energy markets. Recent experiences in the
Chinese energy market provide an example of such a case, where liberalization of the energy market has sometimes drastically changed its direction
influenced by a broader economic policy for stabilizing the domestic economy (Ogawa, 1995).¹²

Regarding Gulf penetration of the Asian energy markets from now on,
the most influential changes are likely to arise from the priority given to
the concern for security of supply. This priority can change the direction of
the energy market from liberalization and deregulation to government

intervention and regulation, which might result in significant constraints on Gulf penetration.

Conclusion

Imports of oil and LNG by Asian countries from outside the region will increase rapidly, as oil and LNG production in Asia ceases to match demand. This will provide opportunities for Gulf oil and gas producers to expand their exports and to penetrate the Asian market. However, Asian governments and industries, worried about security of supply, might try to restrict Gulf penetration of their market, by promoting, for example, energy conservation, alternative energy development, oil and gas production in Asia, and diversification of oil and gas imports from outside the region.

Concern for security of supply has toned down recently, as a result of lower oil prices since 1986, improved ability of oil-importing countries to mitigate impacts of supply disruption, and smaller possibilities of oil supply disruption. Furthermore, liberalization and deregulation are underlying trends in the Asian energy market. Under existing circumstances, policies and strategies to prevent Gulf penetration will not be easily implemented in Asian countries. These policies and strategies might be used in the future, if the security of supply becomes an issue again due to changes in the world energy situation.

Consequently, minimizing concern for security of supply in Asian countries is essential for Gulf oil and gas exporters so that they can realize opportunities to penetrate the Asian market. Gulf oil and gas exporters, now realizing the reciprocal dependency between exporters and importers for mutual prosperity, can minimize concern by their efforts to stabilize (or at least to avoid instability in) the world oil and gas markets, and by their efforts to improve their reliability as energy exporters and investors.

CHAPTER 4

Natural Gas and Gulf Oil: Boon or Bane?

Thomas Stauffer

Introduction

What are the implications of natural gas for OPEC and the Gulf oil producers – is natural gas a boon, or is it a bane? Have the OPEC or Gulf states benefited from their own large gas reserves and more modest production – or
have they suffered from the incursion of natural gas into markets for OPEC
crude oil?

Some benefits from gas – from the producers' perspectives – are readily
apparent. Gas is increasingly consumed in the oil-producing countries for
domestic use, as a fuel and feedstock for industry, and to generate electricity
and produce potable water. It is a unique asset, a low-cost form of indigenous
energy which provides light and water for their populations and the energy
and feedstock for a broad spectrum of basic industries.

Gas use outside of OPEC, however, has resulted in palpable losses for the
OPEC producers. That loss has been twofold. First, competing gas from non-
OPEC (NOPEC) sources has made inroads on oil markets, although, as we
shall show, the impact is less than might be believed. Second – and paradoxically, however – OPEC has suffered competition from itself. It may have lost
sizable wellhead revenues from the commercialization of its own gas
resources, an "externality" which is not readily apparent. The effect of gas has
two dimensions: 1) NOPEC vs OPEC and 2) OPEC vs OPEC. The first is
larger, but the second is significant as well.

This chapter analyzes the gross impact of NOPEC gas production upon
OPEC, highlights the major trends and identifies the key forces. It analyzes
those economic factors which drove the market penetration of gas into the oil
market, and deals with the special case of LNG, an instance where exports by
OPEC states do indeed clearly lead to reduced, not increased, net revenues.
It then examines more generally the economic impact of gas-based industry,
other than LNG.

Global Competition: Oil vs Gas – Market Trends

Natural gas is touted as the "clean fuel for the future." Whatever the future prospects, it is unequivocally clear that natural gas has been the growth fuel over the past 15 years – just as oil was the growth fuel in the decades after the Second World War. The contrast between the production histories of oil and natural gas is clear and stark:

— World oil production was no higher in 1995 than it was in 1979, the year of the second quantum price increase. While growth since 1969, the last year of declining oil prices, has amounted to some 50 percent – 43 vs 66 mmb/d, overall oil production grew at the rate of only 1.4 percent p.a. (1969–94) over the entire period.

— World gas production more than doubled in that same period. Gas production rose from 850 mmtoe in 1969 to 1,875 mmtoe in 1994 – a relative increase of 120 percent, growing at the rate of 3.1 percent p.a.

— Gas and oil shared equally in the absolute increase in output. Annual oil production rose by 1,100 mmtoe in that period, while gas production increased by only a hairbreadth less – 1,025 mmtoe.

— Natural gas is no longer a stepchild of oil – since 1970 it has shared equally in meeting new energy demands.

Gas markets were much more dynamic during the entire period, but the tradeoff between NOPEC gas and OPEC oil intensified after 1979. Gas competed against all oil from all sources – but the market inroads by gas were especially effective *vis-à-vis* OPEC oil. OPEC bore the brunt: its output has fallen and is still 25 percent below its peak level of 31.5 mmb/d. Quite the opposite is true for gas; natural gas output has continued to increase unremittingly since 1970:

— OPEC oil output fell by 25 percent;

— competing gas output rose by almost 50 percent;

— gas captured a significant share of OEPC's oil markets during that period, picking up part of OPEC's historic markets and also preempting an important part of new markets.

Prior to 1970, natural gas had been essentially a local fuel, confined principally to North America, where its economics were dominated by considerations of byproduct costs. Much of the gas in North America was associated gas; it was the unwelcome stepchild of the production of oil. More generally, much of the profit lay in the liquids to be stripped, and the methane itself was sold for decades at low prices as a "quasi-free good."

The industry was localized, an adjunct to large oil production in reasonable proximity to large consumption centers. Seventy percent of all gas in the world was produced in North America, overwhelmingly in just one country, the US. The only other significant producer and consumer was the USSR, but its gas industry was still dwarfed by that in North America. The Gulf produced important quantities, but most of that gas was not commercially usable. It was flared for want of an economic market – the corona from those gas flares illuminated the night in the Upper Gulf for many years after 1945 as increasing volumes were vented and burned off. Then gas was the dangerous byproduct of growing oil production.

Gas became a global fuel with global impact after 1969. The local, co-product character changed irreversibly. Higher oil prices transformed the gas industry and the new price umbrella created a fresh competitor to oil, just as higher oil prices during that period also rescued the nuclear industry and North Sea operations. Hitherto wellhead netbacks for gas had been very low – or negative (offset by NGL revenues) – when the landed price of oil imports was $2/bbl. Two-dollar oil capped the competitive thrust of gas – but $30-oil catalyzed a new, global gas industry.

The competitive picture, however, is rather more complex – the trends in different areas differed, as did the implications for OPEC and competing oil producers. First, much of the increased gas production was in Russia. Russian production increased spectacularly by some 8 mmboe/d. However, little of that gas was traded – most was consumed locally and was not in any useful sense competition for OPEC. The competition, if any, was indirect in the sense that cheap domestic gas permitted the Russians to sustain 2.5 mmb/d of oil exports to hard-currency customers. In the absence of gas, oil exports might have been less, but those volumes did indeed compete with OPEC.

The real impact of Russian gas volumes on OPEC is much less than the aggregate data seem to indicate; an upper bound for the impact of Russian gas is therefore the oil exports which were freed up, plus the actual pipeline exports of gas equivalent to 1.6 mmb/d. Since it could be argued that Russia would have exported that oil irrespective of domestic need, given their greater need for hard currency, the net impact of the very large Russian gas industry upon oil markets may have been only the direct pipeline deliveries.

NOPEC gas, other than Russian production, did compete with OPEC oil. From 1970 onwards, the "competing" production rose by about 5.5 mmboe/d – the estimate of the actual challenge to OPEC oil from NOPEC gas. Thus competing NOPEC gas eroded OPEC markets, year in, year out, by an average of 200,000 b/d per year, accumulating to an increased market share of 5.5 mmb/d by the middle of this decade.

That trend subsumed several subtrends. First, increased production from Canada whittled away about 1.4 mmb/d of oil demand. Most of that occurred in the last eight to nine years, and most of that was not the result of new discoveries of gas, but, rather, the consequence of liberalized regulatory constraints which permitted Canadian producers to export gas at higher rates of depletion. Much of Canada's increased production has come from prior existing reserves. The reserve-to-production ratio (R/P) has plummeted, as the "seed corn" is partly consumed. The recent increase is not readily sustainable.

Second, North Sea producers added 1.6 mmboe/d during the period, much of that coming recently from the UK sector. This resulted primarily from higher, unregulated gas prices in the UK market, and from synergistic effects, discussed below, which compounded incentives for new gas developments.

The US market is more complex. Production had actually fallen through the early 1980s by almost 2.5 mmboe/d, compared with peak production levels of the mid-1970s. This would have led to increased imports of oil except for the sharp recession and price-induced energy conservation. However, since the production nadir was reached in 1986, US gas production has rebounded by the equivalent of 1.5 mmb/d – in spite of low gas prices (see below for discussion of US subsidies for gas).

The inroads against OPEC oil from NOPEC gas have slowed. Except for the subsidized recovery of US gas production, there has been a much slower increase in competing gas supply (excluding Russian gas) since 1986, a not surprising reaction to lower prices and reduced oil exploration. The challenge from gas has been large, but that challenge now seems to have been very much curbed.

Global Competition: Oil vs Gas – Economic Forces

Higher oil prices, creating higher prices at the burner tip against which gas could compete, drove the new gas industry, but the mechanics of those incentives were more complex than the impact of high oil prices upon NOPEC oil. The economics of gas production and marketing are multi-faceted, and five distinct factors have been at work:

— "Tyranny of distance": high oil prices meant that gas could be transported into more distant markets. The window of opportunity was widened.
— "Lucre from liquids": high oil prices meant the value of the byproduct NGLs escalated dramatically.
— "Exploration symbiosis": increased exploration for oil meant not only

more associated gas, found with the oil, but also collaterally more discoveries of gas.

— "Piggyback economics": the economics of replacing production into
existing pipelines are much more favorable than greenfield (or "blue
water") projects.

— Pseudo-economics – subsidies: in the US both the consumption and production of gas have been subsidized in order to reduce oil imports, and
in Japan subsidies were critical for the LNG trade.

The tyranny of distance

Higher oil prices transformed the economics of natural gas. First, higher oil
prices meant higher burner-tip values for gas – and those higher values meant
that the economic reach of gas had been extended. More distant markets
became accessible. The "tyranny of distance" – the high transport cost of gas
per MMBTU – was greatly offset, because it was possible to move gas further.

The cost of transporting natural gas is much higher than moving the same
amount of liquid energy; the transport disability of gas is true both for
pipeline movement and for maritime movement (see Table 4.1).

Table 4.1   Transportation disability: gas versus oil (cents per 1,000 miles per MMBTU)

	Gas	Oil	Gas disability
Pipeline	60	5–10	6–12 times
Marine	10–25	2–3	4–10 times

The transport disability of gas is large – a factor of 4 for short-haul marine
movement, rising to a factor of 12 for long-distance pipeline transport. But
the higher the oil price, the farther out gas is able to reach, either by pipeline
or by cryogenic tanker, because the energy-related costs of shipping are relatively small in relation to the fixed costs. Thus each dollar increase in the
price of oil adds to the marketable distance for gas:

Additional reach (miles per incremental $ per bbl)
Pipeline   250
Tankship   600

Thus $5 per barrel added to the price of oil adds some 1,250 miles to the
competitive range of pipeline gas and 3,000 miles to the competitive range
for LNG shipments.

The principle is quite clear, even though the figures are illustrative because
actual route costs are terrain-, port-, and volume-dependent. Higher oil
prices since 1969, but especially since 1973, have turned shut-in gas into a

major challenge to oil markets, especially markets for OPEC oil. Russian gas exports were at best marginally economic prior to 1973; indeed, it appears possible that only Marxist financial misreckonings of the real cost of pipelines made those exports possible. However, hard-currency gas exports rose from negligible volumes in the 1970s to 1.2 mmboe/d by 1993, thanks to higher prices. Similarly, Troll gas from the North Sea could never have been exported to mainland Europe had higher oil prices not provided the protective umbrella. The full cost of pipelining would have been prohibitive. In both cases higher oil prices were key to transborder marketing of that gas.

"Lucre from liquids"

The second factor is the value of the co-products. Natural gas liquids are critical to the economics of gas production. Almost all gas reservoirs yield some entrained liquids (NGLs) or petroleum gases (LPGs) along with the methane. Associated gas is typically reasonably rich in NGLs – ethane, butane, and heavier hydrocarbons. The liquids content of non-associated gas varies widely. Some gas fields are almost dry, whereas others – such as some of the major gas fields in Algeria – yield high fractions of LPGs and heavier hydrocarbons along with the methane.

The co-products became much more valuable after 1969, which tipped the balance even more favorably toward wet gas production. The stripping and sale of this byproduct has represented an ever more important part of both gross and net revenues from gas production. The importance has risen because the price of the products has risen, dragged up by oil prices, and also because the depth of stripping has intensified, i.e. a larger fraction of those marketable liquids is recovered. The gross value of byproduct NGLs is seen to vary considerably.[1] For "typical" associated gas, the yield of NGLs is circa 0.025 to 0.10 barrels per Mcf, with the average for North America, for example, lying in the range of 0.04–0.06 bbls per Mcf.

Table 4.2   Economic impact of byproduct NGL values

Quality of gas	NGL yield (bbls/Mcf)	Byproduct ($/Mcf)
"Lean"	0–0.025	0–43 cents
"Typical"	0.025–0.10	$0.43–$1.70
"Condensate"	0.10–plus	$1.70–plus

The case of Qatar illustrates the importance of gas liquids. Gas from the North Dome structure reportedly is particularly "wet" – a yield of close to

0.10 bbl/Mcf has been indicated. The impact of NGL recovery upon the project economics is thus profound – the net value of the NGLs, allowing for processing costs, is well over $1/Mcf of dry gas. The NGL value is in fact greater than the probable netback for the methane from the LNG plant (see below).

Similarly, much of Algerian gas is no less rich, and in Algeria gas production is clearly profitable even if the wellhead value were zero. Even an "average" gas stream yields valuable NGLs; at 0.05 bbl/Mcf the byproduct value is about 80–90 cents per Mcf (gross) and 50–75 cents (net).

"Gas is not gas is not gas," to parody the oft-quoted line of Gertrude Stein. The richness of the gas, i.e. its liquids content, is a critical element in the overall economics of gas production. The economics of gas production, therefore, cannot be decoupled from the question of the relative wetness of the gas and the opportunity to commercialize the liquids.

NGLs were especially attractive for OPEC producers because gas liquids were expressly determined to be outside of the quota system after the mid-1980s. Hence production and exports could be increased without unduly complicating intra-OPEC relations. Liquids recovery could be increased without further violating the quotas. Each individual producer thereby benefited, although, as will be discussed below, the overall impact was to reduce OPEC crude exports.

NGLs have been doubly important. NGLs in effect financed much of commercial gas development. But, further, they added considerably to OPEC's gross revenues. As of 1994, OPEC produced almost 2.5 mmb/d of NGLs. Much of those volumes (except for the ethane and some LPG) was exported. Thus the real production of OPEC is almost 10 percent higher than the figures usually reported, which conventionally exclude NGLs.

Symbiotic effects

Third, natural gas was stimulated – and will continue to be stimulated – by a symbiotic effect. This is the spillover impact upon gas exploration of higher oil prices. As oil-targeted drilling increased, more gas was discovered collaterally. Gas production benefited significantly when higher prices, through the mid-1980s, catalyzed an upsurge in oil drilling. Much gas is still found as the incidental result of oil exploration, even though improved seismic techniques and much improved digital analytical methods have made "directionality," i.e. the selective identification of gas vs oil targets, more accurate. Nonetheless, more oil drilling led to more gas discoveries.

For example, fields in the North Sea which would not have been attractive as "standalone" exploration targets could nonetheless be developed quite profitably once discovered in the course of primary searching for oil.

"Piggybank economics"

Another economic factor is an important infrastructural externality – the "piggybank effect." Most of the costs of transporting gas, especially in pipelines, are fixed costs, so that the incremental costs of transporting new volumes of gas can be very low indeed under three important scenarios:

a. Satellite fields: smaller fields can be connected into an existing network even though they would not be developable in their own right. This effect is especially important in the North Sea today.
b. Extended reach: pipelines can be extended backwards to reach ever more remote reserves, again reserves which were otherwise too distant to support development. Since the costs of transporting new gas through the existing system are low, only the costs of the new lines are relevant. This factor dominates the potential scope for gas supplies from the northern North Sea area of the Troll Field itself.
c. Extended thrust ("down-pipe"): the same consideration permits gas to reach farther beyond existing pipelines, since the extended sales may involve only incremental investments. This effect is more complex because of the exponential increases in compressor fuel costs beyond certain levels of line throughput. The real economics of Russian supply to Europe rest upon this consideration – i.e. the incrementality of the costs of exporting additional volumes, piggybacking upon domestic deliveries through the main pipeline system. The main element of costs for the four large-diameter pipelines across CIS-Ural Russia was attributable to serving the domestic markets of western Russia and the (former) satellites. The outreach to Western Europe entailed only marginal costs.

Pseudo-economics: gas subsidies

Off-budget subsidies for both the production and use of natural gas have been extremely important in the US since 1978/79. Today, an important volume of total production enjoys substantial subsidies – equivalent to $3.50 to $6.00 per barrel of oil equivalent. Similarly, much of the new demand for natural gas from the independent power producers ("IPPs") has been subsidized in the sense that consumers are forced to pay rates above market prices for the electricity, which then translates into higher prices and higher demand for gas.

From 1978 onwards, Federal regulations in the US permitted very high priced gas to be rolled in with historically price-controlled, cheap gas. This artifice had the effect of subsidizing prices of new gas which were much higher than could have prevailed in an unregulated market. Special categories of "new" gas qualified for that preferential treatment.

Since then a new set of subsidies has emerged. Through the end of 1992, gas from coal beds ("coal bed methane") and gas from reservoirs deemed to be "tight," i.e. fields with low porosity and/or permeability, qualified for tax credits of 50 and 95 cents per Mcf, respectively. The coal bed methane tax credit was almost as large as the gross wellhead price in certain periods, and both led to significant increased production of subsidized gas. The subsidies, camouflaged as tax credits, attracted little public attention since no appropriation was required. Production of subsidized gas rose to an estimated 3.5 TCF by 1993, almost 20 percent of total marketed volumes.

Technological advances

Technology has played a role as well, but the impact upon oil and gas was comparable, so that better exploration and drilling techniques did not affect the competitive balance as importantly as the above factors. Horizontal drilling, for example, offers cost savings which are essentially proportional for both oil and gas, so that real savings in absolute terms did not affect relative costs as much.

Summary assessment: economic forces

The net effect of higher oil prices, higher NGL values, and the capability to piggyback new gas projects is to alter the relative economics in favor of gas in four key respects:

— Gas can reach into much more distant markets, now that oil prices are higher.
— Exploration for hitherto marginal gas prospects is enhanced because NGL values alone can justify finding and development.
— Replacement of depleting volumes is attractive, thanks to the possibility of piggybacking on existing pipelines, which means that existing gas supplies should exhibit particularly low decline rates.[2]
— Subsidies for production and use of gas in the US added the equivalent of about 1.0–1.25 mmboe/d to US domestic supply, reducing oil imports by the same amount.[3]

Natural gas, once a byproduct of oil production, is now firmly entrenched as a dynamic competitor to oil, thanks to the changes in the relative economics or, in the case of "new" gas in the US or LNG in Japan, important subsidies.

OPEC vs OPEC: the case of LNG

LNG exports have captured a major part of the trans-border gas trade, and that trade is particularly important in this context because it is the clearest example of how OPEC gas competes against OPEC oil. Still worse, from OPEC's collective perspective, is the fact that the revenue trade-off is distinctly unfavorable. High-value oil (at the wellhead) is displaced by gas with lower or even negligible wellhead netback revenues (per barrel of oil equivalent).

The LNG trade today is important only at the margin – by 1994 total LNG traffic had risen to 88 billion m^2 – the energy equivalent of 1.5 mmboe/d. That is a small volume compared either to total oil or to total energy trade. Furthermore, the industry is concentrated. Over three-quarters of that volume originates in OPEC states – Abu Dhabi and Indonesia – while the remainder is exported by three NOPEC producers: Brunei, Malaysia and Australia.

That "margin," however, is important to OPEC and to the Gulf producers, because the 1.5 mmboe/d are directly in competition with the swing volumes of OPEC or Gulf crude oil exports. The displacement effect is close to one-for-one. In Asia, LNG is burned by power plants or larger industrial plants – units which otherwise would have burned heavy fuel oil. Where consumers are connected, the availability of gas reduces demand for kerosene or No. 2 oil, again thereby pushing out oil. In Europe – which takes 25 percent of the total – the LNG is not sold to dedicated customers but is added to the Europe-wide articulated gas grid.[4] However, there, too, much or most of the LNG in effect displaces oil. In the power sector, coal or nuclear plants are used preferentially where allowed or mandated, so that gas displaces oil at the margin. The same is true for industrial users – gas displaces oil.

Overall, LNG competes directly or indirectly with oil, and oil at the margin, of course, in today's markets, is OPEC oil. The collective loss is clear and large. Each tonne of LNG displaces 8.7 barrels of oil.[5] The LNG trade reduces OPEC's gross receipts by $9–10 billion p.a. But the gain to the exporters, taken individually, is comparatively modest. High gross revenues do not necessarily imply high wellhead netback values for the gas itself. This follows because the LNG chain – from the Christmas tree (i.e. wellhead) to the factory gate of the regasification plant – is highly capital intensive. The largest part of the delivered price consists of returns to capital. The return to the resource, to the gas itself, is the netback residual, i.e. the delivered price less the full costs, including returns to capital, of all of the links in the chain.

The effect of liquefaction, transport, and regasification costs upon wellhead netbacks for the gas can be illustrated with reference to two types of LNG export: the short-haul trades vs the long-distance trades (see Table 4.3).

Table 4.3   Short-haul vs long-haul trades

Short-haul	Long-haul
Trinidad–US East Coast	Abu Dhabi–North Asia
Brunei–North Asia	Oman–North Asia
Malaysia–North Asia	Middle East–US
Indonesia–North Asia	Nigeria–US/Europe
Australia–North Asia	
Algeria–Northwest Europe	

The short-haul trades involve distances of circa 3,000 miles while the longer trades are 6,000 miles or even greater. Since shipping LNG is an expensive operation, compared with moving the same amount of energy as crude oil, the netbacks from the longer trades should be less. We can illustrate the effect by working backward and calculating the fully built-up costs, excluding wellhead gas value, for LNG delivered ex-the regasification plant.[6]

Table 4.4   Fully built-up costs (excluding gas price)

	Short-haul ($/Mcf)	Long-haul ($/Mcf)
Liquefaction	1.10	1.10
Transport	0.96	1.80
Terminal and regasification	0.35	0.35
Built-up cost (ex-gas)	2.40	3.25
Reported prices		
Japan	3.00–3.50	3.00–3.50
Europe	2.25	2.25–2.50

The savings on short-haul gas over a longer-haul route are material – the difference in the delivered costs for the regasified LNG is 85 cents per Mcf ($3.25 less $2.40), where the above costs are indicative for greenfield, new projects.

Netback values for gas can be very small. The gas value is at most the difference between the regasified price and the total of the full costs. In the case of long-haul trades into Japan, the Japanese price – $3.00–3.50 – is equal to little more than the full costs exclusive of gas value. That implies a very small or zero netback to the gas itself.

Similarly, for a short-haul trade to Europe, the margin again is low – even though the shipping cost is much less. The margin is still small because the Europeans do not pay any significant premium for LNG, or gas more generally, and the border price in recent years, tied to crude and product prices, is in the range of $2.40 per Mcf. That price is typically 80 cents to $1/Mcf less than the price paid by the Japanese. But that is essentially equal to the fully built-up costs without gas value. Long-distance export of LNG to Japan is feasible only because the Japanese have hitherto been willing to pay unusually high prices for LNG, prices which since the early 1980s have been higher than their fuel-oil equivalent.

One set of routes, however, is potentially profitable. Short-haul gas into Japan can yield a potentially attractive netback gas price. For those routes, such as from Brunei or East Borneo, the difference between full costs and reported prices is close to a dollar per barrel. That leaves a margin for a negotiated netback value for the gas which could be attractive in its own right.

Two further sub-cases must be differentiated – associated vs non-associated gas supplies. In the case of associated gas, the costs of production are nil; the only gas costs incurred for an LNG plant are the modest costs of gathering and pipelining the associated gas to the plant. Thus any margin netted back to the wellhead is essentially pure resource value.

The balance is distinctly less attractive for the case of dedicated non-associated gas, for which finding and development costs must be reckoned in as well. These vary widely from one area to another, but an illustrative range is 20 cents to $1.00 an Mcf, exclusive of any liquids credit. Again, in this case, the margin at the wellhead is narrowed even further when wellhead costs must be borne because the gas is not a byproduct of oil production.

NGL credits are thus the key. The credit depends sensitively upon the wetness of the inlet gas. In the case of the proposed plant in Oman, the liquid yield is projected at almost 0.10 bbls per Mcf, at least in the early years of reservoir exploitation, so that the liquids credit would yield between $1.00 and $1.70 per Mcf – which more than offsets a zero netback for the dry gas itself. The pattern is pervasive; the NGL credits tip the economic balance.

This leads to six conclusions with respect to the net value which a host country can realize from LNG projects:

1. The netback value of dry methane at the wellhead is essentially zero. The value garnered from the gas itself is small or negligible, except for short-haul LNG sales into an overpriced market.

2. The profit lies in the NGLs stripped from a wet inlet gas stream. The byproduct credits yield all or most of the net wellhead value.
3. LNG projects affect OPEC revenues in two ways: a) the LNG itself competes directly with oil in final markets, and b) the NGL's trade-off against oil exports but without large revenue loss.
4. Total OPEC revenues are not affected, net, by the export of NGLs from gas production – NGLs reduce crude oil exports but increase liquid sales revenues by approximately the same amount.
5. OPEC states do lose approximately $150 for every tonne of LNG which is exported, either by their own member states or from NOPEC sources.
6. Total annual losses exceed $9 billion.

It is thus ironic that an ostensibly valuable resource – byproduct or non-associated natural gas – in fact *reduces* rather than enhances OPEC revenues when exported as LNG. The impact of extracted NGLs is a wash – decreased crude exports are balanced by increased NGL exports. However, LNG itself is a deadweight collective loss because it drives out equal amounts of higher-revenue crude oil exports.

There are several winners, however, in spite of the collective loss. Certain states, such as Indonesia, do benefit, but for two reasons which are country-specific: 1) Indonesian LNG enjoys a transportation advantage of almost $1.00/Mcf into Japan, and 2) its crude capacity is limited (Indonesia can barely produce its OPEC quota), so that LNG revenues are genuinely incremental. A further special reason is that Japan has consistently paid an unexplained premium for LNG imports, from which all exporters still benefit. The NOPEC LNG exporters obviously benefit since they have no stake in oil markets and their revenues, even if small, are additive.

OPEC vs OPEC: Energy-intensive Industry

Revenue-enhancing uses of OPEC natural gas

Broadly speaking, OPEC natural gas competes against OPEC oil. The greater the marketed gas production, the greater the loss in gross revenues, as is definitely the case for LNG. The effects of other gas-intensive industries are mixed, and certain very important exceptions must be noted – there are uses of gas within OPEC which unequivocally add domestic value and which have clearly positive impacts upon revenues.

The first such use is gas burned for electricity generation or production of desalinated water in cogeneration plants. That use in no way competes with OPEC or Gulf oil. To the contrary, it represents a real boon because the gas has little or no opportunity cost, on a present value basis, so that the surplus gas is a free good.[7] Thus the producing countries benefit from lower-cost electricity than in most areas where energy carries a high market cost.[8]

A second such use is the large volume of gas which is reinjected into the reservoirs as part of ongoing secondary recovery programs or for recycling in condensate fields (as is widespread in Algeria). Thirty years ago, gas was reinjected for "conservation." Today the practice is better founded, and currently one-quarter of total OPEC gas is returned to the reservoirs, entailing the costs for injection wells and the extensive surface compression facilities. In the case of Algeria, one-half of gross gas production is reinjected; there the purpose is primarily to recycle the gas to maximize the recovery of the light condensates. Elsewhere, the principal objective is to maintain reservoir pressures in order to increase the long-term recovery of oil and also to accelerate that recovery.

Industrial uses as competition to oil

Both of the above uses of gas enhance wellhead revenues; other uses of gas are much more questionable with respect to the impact upon wellhead revenues. Here it is important to distinguish between the returns to capital or foreign factors of production and the return to the gas itself as a depletable resource. The "value" of the gas is the difference between the market value of the output – say fertilizers – and the full economic cost of all inputs to the production of the output. The "resource rent" or value at the wellhead is the residual.

LNG is the simplest example. As noted above, LNG exports yield high gross values when reckoned c.i.f. – but the netback to the methane itself at the wellhead in the exporting countries is very small. Most of the revenues from LNG are attributable to the capital invested downstream from the wellhead, leaving little for the resource.

The economic balance for the other gas or energy-driven industries in the exporting states is more differentiated. Some of the industrial options compete directly with oil, analogous to LNG. Others represent real opportunities to add resource revenue. The major primary options are displayed in Table 4.5.[9]

Table 4.5   Energy-intensive primary industries: the oil producers' options

Basic industry	Competing energy or feedstock
Aluminium	Coal, oil, nuclear, hydro
Cement	Oil, coal (tyres)
Ethylene	Oil, gas
Fertilizers	Oil, gas
Iron (DR)	Coal
Methanol	Oil, gas
Refining	Oil (gas)

Let us first consider two extreme cases. Refining is a case where the projects viewed individually can be quite profitable, given that refining is an energy-intensive process and that the delivered cost of gas as refinery fuel is typically 50 cents/Mcf or less. The fuel cost advantage of such an export refining, enjoying low-cost fuel, is $1–2 per barrel. The fuel cost advantage is as large as, or higher than, the typical, industry-wide gross refining margin. The project-level competitive advantage is thus formidable.[10]

OPEC as a whole, however, loses on each exported barrel of products. The "loss" for export refining results from displacement. Any barrel which would have been refined abroad would have required between 0.03 and 0.12 barrels of oil-fuel input to yield the barrel of product. There is a range of displacement values because refineries vary in their complexity, i.e. in the intensity of processing or conversion, and the fuel requirement is higher the "whiter" the product slate. The more sophisticated the refinery, the greater the fuel use, i.e. the more complex the refinery or the greater the degree of conversion, the greater is the revenue yield from a barrel, but the greater also is the fuel consumption per barrel of product.

That refinery fuel which is "saved" would have been exported from OPEC. The negative externality from export refining, where natural gas is used for refinery fuel, can be estimated and is large. If the competing refinery outside of OPEC had used 0.08 bbls per barrel of product – an example of a refinery of medium complexity – the externality cost is some $1.28 to $2.00 per barrel of product. Thus a 500,000 b/d export refinery might be profitable when audited in isolation, but it would cost the swing producers, or OPEC in the aggregate, between $200 and 300 million per year in lost wellhead revenues due to the displaced refinery fuel which might otherwise have been exported had the processing been done abroad.

The opposite case is that of sponge iron production, using natural gas as fuel and the reducing agent. Direct reduction plants ("DR") are widespread throughout the OPEC states and the Gulf (Bahrain, Qatar, Saudi Arabia, etc.). It is these plants in particular which triggered the term for the Gulf – "the new Ruhr without water." The Midrex or HyL processes for producing sponge iron are well established, and gas, supplied to such specially designed facilities, is an alternative to expensive and bulky metallurgical-grade (coking) coal used in conventional steel mills. Thus local production of such low-grade steel products, or their exportation, does not compete with oil, because the alternative fuel-feedstock is coal, not oil.[11]

Aluminium smelters are an example where the impact is unclear. Each kilogram of aluminium ingot requires 13.5 to 17 kwhr of electricity, the equivalent of 22 to 29 barrels of oil equivalent primary energy into a power plant. The displacement effect, however, depends upon what type of power generation is displaced by the ingot exported from an oil-producing country. In Japan, the marginal supply of power was oil-fired, so oil was displaced. When the Japanese cut back or closed down aluminium smelters, they reduced correspondingly the demand for domestically generated electricity which, at the margin, came from oil-fired stations. Elswhere, where coal or hydro or nuclear power are the alternatives for baseload supply, no oil might be displaced.

The externality cost, or displacement effect, of an aluminium smelter thus varies. It ranges between zero – where the exportation competes with non-oil sources of electricity – and a cost of $350/tonne of ingot up to $560/tonne, where the electricity "saved" would have been fired with oil. Thus, in the extreme case, the displacement cost of a 300,000 tonne per year smelter would lie between $100 and 150 million p.a. in terms of lost wellhead revenues, less the value of the gas embedded in the product. The gross "loss" would be reduced by perhaps 20 percent if the netback to the gas is about 50 cents/Mcf. The offset would be still less if the smelter were not highly profitable.

It does not follow that such projects are uneconomic. First, a collective cost is not a national cost. Second, longer-term resource conservation, given that the alternative would be flaring or uneconomic reinjection, is itself a recognized goal. Third, the linkage benefits from the industrial projects are understood to be large and positive, although extensive studies are not available, so that the implications for creating a technological and industrial base, with all of the well-argued spillover effects, are generally understood.

Nonetheless, some OPEC gas – perhaps half of that marketed to industry – displaces OPEC oil. The net displacement effect is thus real, but can only be estimated, absent a more comprehensive survey. The order of magnitude export displacement is approximately 1 mmb/d, i.e. the gas-based export industries will have reduced OPEC's *collective* exports by that amount. Those lost exports entail a gross reduction in oil export revenues of $15–18 million per day, or $5–6 billion per year.[12] If real wellhead revenues from the embedded gas are, say, 50 cents/Mcf, that is the gas transfer price which is charged in some areas, then an illustrative value for the net resource revenue loss is $4–5 billion per year. Again, one must offset the tangible and intangible benefits from the direct and induced industrial development against that tangible loss.

Summary

Natural gas has become a major factor impacting on OPEC or the Gulf states.

Globally, growing gas production in NOPEC areas has cut severely into OPEC's export revenues. The volumetric loss is at least 4.5 mmb/d – after deducting "non-competing" gas production. Head-to-head gas production, from OPEC and NOPEC, has thus carved almost $30 billion annually from OPEC's collective receipts.

OPEC's gas production also contributed to its loss. Paradoxically, the commercialization of OPEC's own gas resources has either added no net revenues, or possibly even reduced net revenues. Local gas production in the Gulf has clearly promoted economic development and added to the quality of life – but simultaneously that gas has added little or nothing to government revenues. The fraternal competition of OPEC gas vs OPEC oil can only be estimated – the loss of oil volumes is circa 2 mmb/d. The additional net revenue loss lies in the vicinity of $10 billion p.a.

The benefit is apparent. Local gas production is cheap; when stripped of valuable NGLs, that gas is produced at all but nil cost. Today, it provides the fuel and feedstock for competitive energy-intensive industries. These industries, based on surplus gas supplies, otherwise non-commercializable, have helped transform the host economies by adding value to the raw material resources. That gas also permits cheap water and electricity, a special boon in today's world where energy prices are a particular burden in the developing world.

The first cost is also apparent. Expanding production of gas outside of OPEC has carved out a growing share of energy markets. Gas competes head-on against OPEC oil. Now priced against current oil values, "NOPEC" gas production has exploited economies of scale and incremental economics to become a formidable competitor to OPEC oil.

High oil prices since 1973 provided a protective umbrella for gas competition, from which gas particularly benefited *vis-à-vis* oil:

— The "tyranny of distance" was mitigated: gas could extend its reach out into more distant markets.
— The "lucre from liquids" permitted profitable operation even with negative wellhead netbacks, because byproduct NGL values were much higher.
— "Exploration symbiosis" resulted in gas fields being discovered thanks to the heightened search for oil.
— "Piggyback economics" became ever more important, since replacement supplies were grafted onto pipelines or infrastructure at only incremental costs.
— 'Pseudo-economics" was important in the US market, where both production and consumption of new gas was heavily subsidized, albeit "off
  • budget."[13]

Competition to oil from gas is particularly invasive. The costs of sustaining gas supply are relatively low, once the front-end costs of pipelines or infrastructure have been incurred. Thus competition from gas is especially persistent and hard to displace through market forces. Only in mature, or geriatric, producing provinces, such as the US, is the balance less favorable to gas. Otherwise, once gas is ensconced, lower oil prices can discourage expansion, but replacement investment remains quite attractive.

New technologies, such as 3-D seismic studies and horizontal drilling, cut the costs for both oil and gas, but gas benefited additionally due to substantial subsidies in the US and the symbiotic effects of higher oil prices upon byproduct values (NGLs) and exploration activity.

The second challenge is less obvious – OPEC competes with itself. OPEC gas production has fueled OPEC's domestic economies, but the net effect upon total hydrocarbon revenues has been modest – possibly even negative. OPEC gas competes directly with OPEC oil – BTU for BTU. For example, LNG exports yield little net revenue for the methane at the wellhead (except for NGL credits), but compete directly against OPEC oil at the burner tip. OPEC's own LNG exports reduce total revenue by about $5 milliard a year and the total LNG trade by $8–9 billion.

Similarly, exports of ethylene-based products, derived from extracted ethane, largely displace naphtha crackers based on OPEC oil in the importing country. Exports of ammonia or urea fertilizers also displace naphtha-based plants abroad, so there is no net overall gain, in terms of resource revenues, because low-valued gas is replacing high-valued oil. Thus some of the industrial uses of gas, while catalyzing backward, lateral, and forward linkages and promoting overall economic development, actually reduce real revenues. Other industries, such as direct-reduction steel (DR), unequivocally add to resource revenues (rents). Aluminium smelters are intermediate; they add to resource revenues where the competing source of power is coal- or nuclear-generated, but reduce revenues where oil-fired generation is displaced.

Broadly speaking, energy-based industrialization results in a net reduction in hydrocarbon revenues for OPEC or the Gulf as a whole, even though individual exporters may show modest net gains from gas commercialization. That overall loss, however, can be viewed as an acceptable trade-off for the positive linkages and infrastructural advantages associated with gas-based industrial development.

The economic balance is mixed. The intangible benefits are clearly positive – cheap domestic gas is an important boon to OPEC's domestic economies. The tangible benefits are negative – gas is a double bane. On the one hand, NOPEC gas competes head-on with OPEC oil, displacing OPEC exports. On the other hand, much of OPEC's own gas production, used as LNG or in industries such as fertilizers, also competes directly and indirectly with OPEC oil. The competition from gas has been formidable, and its dynamic differs from that of oil so that it may continue to be difficult for OPEC to challenge that competition, even if present price levels prevail.

CHAPTER 5

The Economics of Petroleum
in the Former Soviet Union

Michael C. Lynch[1]

Introduction: Impact

Under Lenin, we were taught that socialism is the shortest road from capitalism to communism. Under Gorbachev, we realized that socialism is the
longest, most painful, road from capitalism to capitalism (Russian joke).

Sometimes it is hard to remember that Russia is still the third largest oil
producer in the world and the sixth largest exporter.[2] Historically, both
imperial Russia and the Soviet Union repeatedly affected the world oil market as new discoveries or export streams put pressure on prices, often unex-
pectedly. But in the past few years, it has been the collapse of production in
the former Soviet Union (FSU) that, quantitatively, has been the second
largest development in the market, surpassed only by the collapse in FSU
consumption.[3] The net effect on the oil market, obviously, has been relatively
small, although the accompanying uncertainty about exports has magnified
the impact of actual changes.

As in other areas of oil market analysis, optimistic and pessimistic views of
the situation have clashed. The optimists (by this definition) see the FSU as
a region of abundant resources, with many enormous oil fields, likely to
recover and increase its exports, perhaps to levels higher than in the mid-
1980s. The pessimists point to the fact that the industry is in disrepair, with
large quantities of oil lost from poor production practices, and massive
amounts of equipment depreciating prematurely as a result of insufficient
maintenance.

As always, the future remains difficult to foresee. Will all of the deals
now in limbo go through and send huge new torrents of oil to the world
market? Will economic reform lead to a boom that will bring forth tens of

millions of new drivers? Or will the economy continue to muddle along, with individual actors fighting so strenuously over the spoils of oil riches that investment (and production, and exports) are retarded for years and decades to come?

The purpose of this chapter is to analyze the potential long-term impact of the FSU oil industry on global oil markets. It will argue that the difficulties the industry faces are largely short-term or transient, or policy-related and therefore surmountable, and that the presence of large, low-cost resources will determine the industry's long-term behavior. Although the industry faces a number of policy and regulatory problems, including the need for refinement of the new petroleum legislation and the uncertainty about the outcome of the presidential elections, these are all highly volatile factors. The taxes imposed on the petroleum industry have been repeatedly revised in the past few years and will undoubtedly be so many more times before the end of the decade. The focus on resource economics is more valuable for long-term analysis, since taxes and legislation can be modified to accommodate the economics of production, while the reverse is much less true.

FSU Oil Forecasts

In this section, current projections of the FSU oil situation will be reviewed. The historical forecasting record will be considered, to put current projections in context.

Current expectations

Expectations for FSU production have changed recently, with much more optimism about future developments. Specifically, there is fairly strong consensus that FSU/EE production[1] will continue to decline for a period, then recover. In Table 5.1, the forecasts of the major organizations are presented. While the general trends are in agreement, bear in mind that even discarding outliers, disagreement over production in the year 2010 remains on the order of 2 mb/d.

The disparity is much greater for oil consumption (Table 5.2), although again the trend is for weakness over the next few years before post-2000 recovery. Since many forecasters combine FSU and Eastern European oil consumption, Table 5.2 also shows the average annual growth rate from 2000 to 2010, i.e., after the current transition period. Even here, the difference is quite noticeable: between the IEA and US DOE alone, the growth rates range from 2.8 percent to 4.2 percent per year.[5]

Table 5.1   FSU production forecasts, mb/d

Forecaster	1990	1991	1992	1994	1995	2000	2005	2010	2020
Dienes, Dobozi, Radetzki (1994)									
Shock therapy					7.8	9.2	11.0		
Gradual reforms					7.8	9.0	10.4		
Reform impasse					7.6	8.6	10.0		
From Watkins									
Davies (1994)							11.5		
Wishful thinking							5.5		
Chaos							8.2		
Troika (1993)							6.2		
World Bank (1992)									
Reform in 1992					7.8				
Reform in 1993					6.3				
IEA									
1994 World Energy Outlook	9.6					7.7	8.6	10.3	
1995 World Energy Outlook									
Capacity constraint case				7.5		7.7		10.7	
Energy savings case				7.5		7.5		10.0	
1995 supply outlook									
Rising price to $28			8.9		6.8	7.4	9.0	10.4	
Flat price			8.9		6.8	7.2	8.6	9.7	
CERI (1994)				7.2	6.8	6.2	8.6		
From DOE (1995):									
DOE (1995)			9.2			8.9		11.4	
PEL (1994)						7.7		9.4	
PIRA (1994)						8.5			
DRI (1994)						8.1		10.0	
NWS (1994)						7.7			
From IEW 1995:									
PREM (1995)	11.4					9.2		10.7	
MERGE (1994)	11.2					12.3		16.3	21.1
Lynch (1994)	11.4					12.0		14.6	17.8
EIA (1994)	11.0					8.2		10.6	
GRREF (1993)	11.5					11.2		9.7	8.0
ITREF (1993)	11.2					11.0		13.2	14.8
SIOPT (1993)	11.2					7.6		7.6	6.8
SIREA (1993)	11.2					6.8		7.2	6.6
IIYSB (1992)	11.4					11.0		10.5	9.5
IIYSL (1992)	11.4					11.0		10.5	8.5

Notes: DOE (1995), PEL (1994) and NWS (1994) include E. Europe.

IEW *World Energy Outlook* (1994) and (1995) include E. Europe, but IEA 1995 supply outlook does not.

CERI is CIS. PEL, PIRA, DRII and NNWS all from DOE (1995).

Table 5.2 Soviet Union/FSU consumption

Forecaster	1990	1991	1992	1994	1995	2000	2005	2010	2020	Annual Growth, 2000 to 2010 (%)
Dienes, Dobozi, Radetzki (1994)										
Shock therapy	8.3				6.6	5.8	6.2			
Gradual reforms	8.3				7.8	6.8	6.6			
Reform impasse	8.3				7.8	7.6	7.0			
IEA, *World Energy Outlook*										
1994 edition										
Rising price to $28	8.24					6.12		7.82		2.5
1995 edition										
Capacity constraint case				4.8		5.7		7.9		3.3
Energy savings case				4.8		5.4		7.1		2.8
From DOE (1995):										
US DOE (1995)			7.8			6.1		9.2		4.2
PEL (1994)						6.4		10.1		4.7
PIRA (1994)						7.1		7.4		0.4
DRI (1994)						4.5				
NWS (1994)						6.6		5.0		−2.7
CERI (1994)				4.9	4.6	4.8	6.2			
From IEW 1995:										
GRREF (1993)	11.57					11.70		11.06	10.05	−0.6
PREM (1995)	8.50					6.20		7.10		0.6
MERGE (1994)	8.46					9.48		5.01	5.05	−6.2
Lynch (1994)	8.05					6.58		6.92	7.64	0.5
EIA (1994)	8.22					6.08		7.34		1.9
ITREF (1993)	8.37					5.74		5.88	5.79	0.2
SIOPT (1993)	7.74					5.40		5.14	5.00	−0.5
SIREA (1993)	7.74					4.90		4.56	4.60	−0.7
IITYSB (1992)	8.80					8.70		8.50	8.50	−0.2
IIYSL (1992)	8.80					8.70		7.50	6.50	−1.5
IEA (1994)	8.18					6.12		7.82		2.5
AMOCH (1993)	8.14					7.00		9.00		2.5
AMOCL (1993)	8.14					6.20		7.50		1.9
WECA (1993)	7.56								6.96	−0.3 *
WECE (1993)	7.56								7.10	−0.2
WECE (1993)	7.56								7.64	0.0
WECC (1993)	7.56								4.60	−1.6
Mean	8.29					7.14		7.18	6.62	0.1
Mean excl. GRREF	8.09					6.76		6.85	6.31	

*1990–2020

Table 5.3　Soviet Union/FSU exports, mb/d

Forecaster	1990	1991	1992	1994	1995	2000	2005	2010	2020
Pagliaresi (1993)						4.0	7.0		
Dienes, Dobozi, Radetzki (1994)									
Shock therapy	3.1				1.2	3.4	4.8		
Gradual reforms	3.1				0.0	2.2	3.8		
Reform impasse	3.1				−0.2	1.0	3.0		
CERI				2.3	2.2	1.4	2.4		
From IEW 1995:									
GRREF (1993)	−0.1					−0.5		−1.3	−2.1
PREM (1995)	2.9					3.0		3.6	
MERGE (1994)	2.8					2.9		11.3	16.1
Lynch (1994)	3.3					5.4		7.7	10.2
ITREF (1993)	2.9					5.3		7.3	9.0
SIOPT (1993)	3.5					2.2		2.5	1.8
SIREA (1993)	3.5					1.9		2.6	2.0
IIYSE (1992)	2.6					2.3		2.0	1.0
Mean	2.7					2.8		4.5	5.4
Mean excl.									
GRREF	3.1					3.3		5.3	6.7
FSU/EE exports									
IEA									
World Energy Outlook									
1994		1.1				0.6	0.7	0.3	
World Energy Outlook									
1995									
Capacity constraints				1.4		0.4		0.6	
Energy savings				1.4		0.6		0.8	
DOE (1995)			1.4			2.8		2.2	

Note: CERI is for CIS.

Needless to say, projections of oil exports (crude plus products), as the residual of production and consumption, vary enormously (Table 5.3). The IEA, which is very optimistic about the recovery of consumption, expects net exports (after E. European consumption) to be marginal in the long run. Most others, however, anticipate a significant increase, particularly after the year 2000.

Past forecasting

Given the enormous uncertainties in making any predictions about the future, it is always important to evaluate a forecast in comparison to earlier projections, partly because it allows one to see whether expectations are relying on previous, discredited arguments.[6] The next section reviews general lessons from past forecasting, and discusses their applicability to the current FSU situation.

General forecasting lessons

Before considering what forecasters are predicting for FSU oil and gas, it would be valuable to recall some of the lessons gleaned from the track record of energy forecasting.[7] As we shall see, there are strong reasons to suspect that past failures are being repeated. The general forecasting lessons are:

1. Consensus and reliability are not correlated; or more appropriately, forecasters are afraid to deviate from the consensus.
2. Forecasters tend to be conservative, particularly in the sense of either seeking consensus or extrapolating from past trends and behavior.
3. Forecasters often ignore basic economic facts, particularly the importance of price.
4. Predictions often suffer from the "horizon effect" where behavior is assumed to change beyond the immediate, foreseeable future.
5. Forecasters tend to focus on large-scale developments, and do not see the effect of large numbers of minor actions, especially on the supply side.[8]

The lessons for oil and gas forecasting specifically are:

1. price forecasts tend to be too high, supply too low;
2. economics and especially the role of price tend to be underestimated;
3. the lead times for developments are often exaggerated; and
4. forecasters focus excessively on depletion effects, overlooking or minimizing the ability of companies to reduce costs and increase supply.

Previous expectations

Before 1985, the USSR probably will find itself not only unable to supply oil to Eastern Europe and the West on the present scale but also having to compete for OPEC oil for its own use ... We estimate that the Soviet Union and Eastern Europe [will require a minimum of 3.5 million b/d of imported oil by 1985]. At worst, slumping production could lead to import requirements as large as 4.5 million b/d. (CIA, *The International Energy Situation: Outlook to 1985*, April 1977b).

The CIA's 1977 report on Soviet oil production[9] is now considered one of the classic examples of energy forecasting mistakes. It correctly foresaw that poor oilfield practices (particularly early, excessive waterflooding) would lead to a collapse in production, but also assumed no change in investment (which delayed the collapse for many years). In its 1977 energy forecast, quoted above, the CIA extrapolated growing Soviet oil demand to conclude that by the mid-1980s, the Soviet Union would be a major importer of oil.[10] In fact, of course, exports continued to grow for another decade, reaching 2.2 mb/d, a 1.1 mb/d increase.

For many years, however, the CIA reports dominated projections of the Soviet oil situation, and the great majority of forecasts called for oil exports from the Centrally Planned Economies (CPE, which includes China and E. Europe, since the Soviet Union was rarely considered on its own at that time) to decline to zero as seen in Figure 5.1, the evolution of US DOE's forecast. Figure 5.2 is a compilation of forecasts for 1990, collected and published by DOE, and the same problem is evident. The fact that all of the forecasts are too low is a classic example of forecasting bias, in this case, pessimism about possible supply.

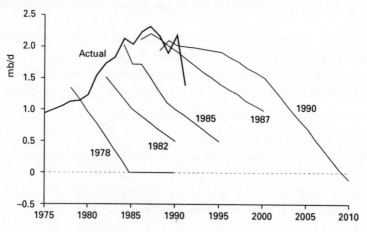

Fig. 5.1   DOE forecast of CPE exports

In reality, most of these early projections were not forecasts but assumptions, reflecting the inability of even the most sophisticated organization to understand and predict developments in the Soviet Union given the many data and political uncertainties.

Lately, however, there has been an increasing effort to analyze and project energy developments in the FSU. Lynch (1995a) reviewed these and found

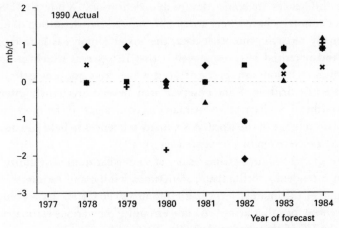

Fig. 5.2 Forecasts of CPE oil exports for 1990

that they tended to be much too conservative, predicting gradual declines in production and consumption rather than the rapid collapses which actually occurred. This is an example of the aforementioned extrapolation (lesson 2 above) and reinforces the idea that the situation may change abruptly again, and that forecasters are not sufficiently sensitive to this.

Conclusion: accept bullish consensus with caution

Overall, then, most forecasters are optimistic about the recovery of FSU oil production and demand, though few see it happening soon. Most experts seem to think that oil exports will continue to be robust, and even to increase after 2000. However, expert opinion is not highly reliable, has tended to seek consensus, and is typically conservative, especially about oil supply.

The primary determinants of the FSU's oil situation over the long run will be the amount and cost of oil available. (Also, these issues are more amenable to analysis than policy decisions.) The next two sections will address resource abundance and costs, respectively.

Resources

Obviously, in order to be produced, oil must exist beneath the ground. Unfortunately, knowledge about resources is always uncertain and imprecise, although many observers fail to recognize this. Certainly, the usual caveats about misinterpreting the nature of petroleum resources (and data) are, if anything, magnified when dealing with the former Soviet Union, especially given the differences in nomenclature and definition. While the US and many other countries have a very strict and conservative definition of proved reserves, many reporting no other data, the Soviet Union has long reported probable and potential reserves as well – that is, reserves which geological and statistical techniques suggest exist, but which have not been definitively demonstrated by drilling. Some observers may have inadvertently interpreted the very liberal Soviet reserve estimates as equivalent to the more conservative, Western usage of the word. Also, many references to field size describe oil-in-place, not recoverable, or proved reserves[11]

But even global resource estimates are of somewhat dubious validity, having shown a tendency to fluctuate, sometimes wildly, and estimates of the FSU's resources (ultimately recoverable resources, or URR), have tended to grow like those for other areas.[12] As one example, the various estimates produced by the USGS (Masters et al., 1983–94) at different times are shown in Figure 5.3; the continuity of authorship should minimize definitional or measurement differences. Yet even here, we can see that the estimates of the FSU's URR have grown by 2.7 percent per year over the past decade.

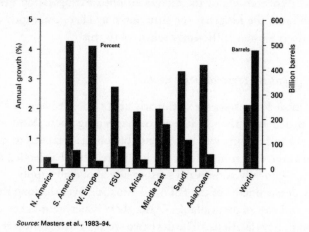

Source: Masters et al., 1983–94.

Fig. 5.3   Rate of growth in oil resource estimates

Resource estimates: URR

Two things are suggested by the resource data in Table 5.4. First, although the FSU and Russia are hardly immature oil provinces, they remain quite abundant, with proved and undiscovered oil twice that of the US (although a fraction of some Middle Eastern countries). Overall, the proportion of the endowment which has been discovered to date (including past production) is still significantly below that of the US. Indeed, Russia is closer to the Middle

East and the UK than to the US in terms of its purported resource base which has been already produced.[13]

Table 5.4 Petroleum resources of the former Soviet Union (billion barrels)

	1992 Production (tb/d)	Cumulative production	Proved reserves	Inferred reserves	Undiscovered resources			Total endowment	R/P
					Mean	Low	High		
Armenia	0.0	0.0	0.0	0.0	6.4				
Azerbaijan	224.7	7.3	1.3	1.7	3.6	2.0	9.0	13.9	15.9
Belarus	41.1	0.6	0.3	0.3	0.2	0.1	0.5	1.4	20.0
Kazakhstan	49.0	3.0	3.3	13.7	26.0	14.0	89.0	46.0	184.4
Kyrgyzstan	2.7	0.1	0.2	0.1	0.6	0.4	1.6	1.0	200.0
Tajikistan	2.7	0.1	0.1	0.2	0.3	0.2	0.5	0.7	100.0
Turkmenistan	98.6	5.1	1.5	1.0	5.0	2.0	10.0	12.6	41.7
Ukraine	98.6	1.9	0.6	0.5	1.1	0.4	3.4	4.1	16.1
Uzbekistan	54.8	0.4	0.3	1.0	3.0	2.0	8.0	4.7	15.0
Russia	7,972.6	90.0	49.0	51.0	68.0	40.0	171.0	258.0	16.8
US	7,171.0	157.0	20.2	62.1	30.3	23.5	39.6	269.6	7.7
UK	1,950.0	11.2	4.4	10.7	13.9			40.2	6.2
Middle East	18,295.0	185.0	663.0		51.0			899	99.3

Source: Riva, Jr., 1994.
Notes: US from API, citing USGS 1989. Armenia from OGJ 5/22/95, Wheaton et al. Estimate for Armenia may be overstated due to definitional differences. Middle East: Masters, 1984 for URR, DeGolyer MacNaughton for cumulative production (1918–93); and IESS for reserves.

But note also that only Russia and Azerbaijan, of the republics of the FSU which are considered to have significant petroleum resources, have been heavily exploited according to this measure. Kazakhstan in particular appears very much underexploited. Given its isolation from world oil markets and the sour nature of Tengiz crude in particular, this might be considered rational, but it may also reflect the bureaucratic nature of the Soviet decision-making, which did not optimize drilling investment, as Gustafson (1990) describes.

Other evidence of abundance

Other geological data exist which illustrate the potential of the FSU in at least an approximate way, including field size, well density, and productivity. Comparing these indicators with Western data, of course, can result in mis-perceptions due to definitional problems and caution must be exercised.

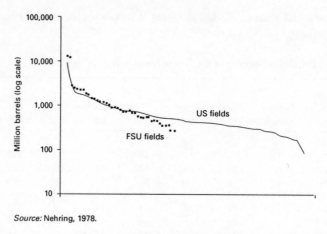

Source: Nehring, 1978.

Fig. 5.4   Field size distribution

Field size

One useful source is Nehring (1978), who lists the world's giant fields by country and estimated ultimate recoverable reserves. Figure 5.4 shows the FSU fields compared to the US's, ranked by size on a logarithmic scale. Since discovered oil fields decline in size gradually in a given region, the curve suggests the likely size of future discoveries. In this case, it appears as if the FSU curve is declining much more rapidly than the US's; however, inferior geological prospects is only one possible explanation. Still, even a pessimistic reading of this graph implies that there are numerous, undiscovered fields in the FSU, a theory supported by other evidence.

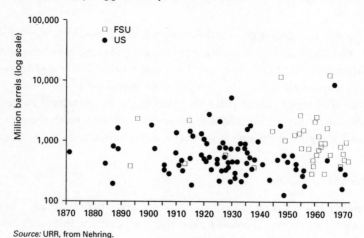

Source: URR, from Nehring.

Fig. 5.5   Comparison of US/FSU fields

For one thing, these estimates contain a subjective element. As Lynch (1995c) showed, even for US fields, Nehring's estimates have proven too low, despite the superior knowledge of US reservoir characteristics. And since most of the FSU fields are of relatively recent vintage, as Figure 5.5 shows, and thus will have grown less than the more mature US fields, it seems highly likely that their sizes are understated relative to US fields.

Given Table 5.4's estimates of total FSU resources as approximating the US's in size, then the FSU field size curve should extend in a similar manner to the US curve, meaning that there are many, very large, undiscovered fields yet to be found.[14] And a more recent listing of field size, shown in Table 5.5, estimated much greater recoverable reserves for some of the giant fields than Nehring's 1978 report, suggesting that the FSU field size curve in Figure 5.4 is in fact understated, perhaps seriously so.

And the large fields certainly are present in the FSU. Table 5.6 is a listing of the major undeveloped fields being proposed or offered for development in Siberia, the Russian Far East, and the daughter republics. Most fields dwarf anything being found in any other region outside the Middle East. For example, the last time a billion barrel oil field was found in the lower-48 United States was 1948 and even in Alaska there are only two producing fields above that size, Kuparak River and Prudhoe Bay. Even though the Russian oil industry has a less constrained definition of field size, it is clear that a number of fields above a billion barrels remain unexploited.

Table 5.5   Growth in FSU giant oil fields

Name	Date of discovery	Estimated resources: Nehring (1978)	Estimated resources: Dienes et al. (1994)	Ratio
Samotlor	1966	13,000	23,461	1.80
Mamontovo	1965	1,750	4,262	2.44
Sovetskoye	1962	1,250	1,392	1.11
Pravdinsk	1964	950	1,590	1.67
Pokachev	1970	800	1,667	2.08
W. Surgut	1962	730	1,392	1.91
Fedorov	1971	600	5,433	9.05
North Varyegan	1971	600	664	1.11
Vat'yegan	1971	500	1,914	3.83
Totals		20,180	41,775	2.07

Table 5.6   FSU size of undeveloped fields

Area	Field	Size mil. bbls.	Notes/Source
Yamai-Nenets Okrug	Taz	4,015	Proved and probable. OGJ 8/14/95, p.17.
	Beregovy	601	Proved and probable. OGJ 8/14/95, p.17.
	E. Taz	337	Proved and probable. OGJ 8/14/95, p.17.
	Salekapt	511	Proved and probable. OGJ 8/14/95, p.17.
	Stakhanov	366	Proved and probable. OGJ 8/14/95, p.17.
	Priobskoye		
Tyumen	N. Gubinskoye	30	OGJ 4/12/93.
Khanti-Mansi	North Priol	12,410	Proved, probable, and possible. OGJ 8/10/92, p.21.
	Salim	13,870	Proved, probable, and possible. OGJ 8/10/92, p.21.
	Novoportov	5,548	Proved, probable, and possible. OGJ 8/10/92, p.21.
Tyumen	Vankorskoye	1,080	OGJ 7/26/93
Russian Far East	Piltun-Astoksoy	550	WSJ 10/2/94.
Kazakhstan	Tengiz	4,500	OGJ 6/20/94.
	Karaganchak	1,900	PIW 3/6/95.
Azerbaijan	Azeri/Chiraq/Gu	3,000	OGJ 11/8/93
Uzbekistan	Kokdumalak	1,000	OGJ 1/30/95, p.39.
Projects/aggregations			
Timan-Pechora	11 fields	2,400	WSJ 12/8/93.
Kazakhstan	67 offshore	3,000	OGJ 5/15/95.

Well density and productivity

Well density is another indication of the maturity of a province, and while the FSU's level of nearly 7 wells drilled per 100 square km of sedimentary basis is substantially above the Middle East level of 0.5, it is well below the US figure of 33 in 1970, the year that lower-48 production peaked. This suggests that the FSU's production peak is well into the future, and probably higher than the 1987 level of 12.7 mb/d.

Well productivity, despite the poor engineering practices in the FSU, remains significant. In Table 5.7, estimates of 1990 well productivity are shown for Russia and W. Siberia, compared to the US.[15] In general, although Siberian well productivity and returns to drilling have been described as poor, they remain well above the US average.

More importantly, it is logical to expect that better management will raise productivity, more than offsetting any effect of depletion for some time. Shpilman and Brekhuntsov (1992) for example, said that well productivity could be increased by 50–100 percent with appropriate technology and management. Shultz (1993) observed that at the Komi Arctic Oil joint venture, wells drilled using Western technology produce at levels of as much as 3 tb/d, raising average field productivity from 350 b/d/well to 900 b/d/well. And the Upper Vozey joint venture is said to have experienced a doubling of well productivity from the application of Western technology.[16] Naturally, these may be exceptional cases, but they suggest that FSU well productivity is not only relatively high, but likely to increase substantially in coming years.[17]

Table 5.7 Well productivity, 1990

Well productivity	% of production Russia	W. Siberia
>730 b/d	0.1	
365–730 b/d	0.6	9.4
182–365 b/d	34.4	44.7
36–182 b/d	45.5	45.9
<36 b/d	11.4	
	B/D/Well	
Alaska	1,209.7	
California	22.0	
Colorado	13.0	
Oklahoma	3.0	
Texas	10.2	

Source: FSU data from Dienes, Dobozi, and Radetzki, p.43. US data from American Petroleum Institute Basic Petroleum Data Book, 1993.
Note: US stripper well production 1990: 462,823 wells, avg. 2.2 b/d, 13.9% total production.

The availability of so many undeveloped fields in the FSU and their relatively high productivity supports the hypothesis that resources remain abundant and that the estimates of undiscovered oil are probably significantly understated. This evidence hardly allows us to generate a precise production curve for the FSU, but it certainly suggests that the resource availability and economics are so favorable as to allow a recovery of production, possibly exceeding former record levels.

Economics of Production

Since the late 1980s, pessimists have focused on the collapsing performance of the FSU oil industry, including the need to repair or replace many of the oil pipelines and other infrastructure, falling productivity of existing wells, and

declining returns to drilling, as well as the enormous losses from poor management and engineering practices in the Soviet era. Numerous analyses have argued
that costs are high and soaring, and some have even questioned the economic via-
bility of large-scale investment in FSU, particularly Siberian, oil fields.[18]

Certainly, large-scale oil reserves have been lost due to excessive waterflooding
and other practices in the Soviet era,[19] and there is no question that large amounts
must be spent to restore infrastructure and for environmental remediation.
However, the lost oil should be considered lost, and not relevant to current development costs. Repairing infrastructure and correcting environmental degrada-
tion will go forward with or without new project developments, and should be
considered as externalities. New projects may be forced to carry some of those
costs, but only if the rents are large enough to accommodate them. Pipeline and
environmental costs are never more than a fraction of current world prices,
regardless of how large the absolute capital expenditures may be, as shown by
Dienes et al. (1994) and the IEA (1994c).[20] Thus, unless oil production is only
marginally profitable, all of the various other costs (pipeline repair, refinery
upgrading, etc.) are irrelevant. The crucial question is: what will future production costs be?

Analytical difficulties

While prices are fairly well known through official sources, average costs and
their breakdown can only be approximated in very rough terms. (*Russian Energy
Prices, Taxes and Costs 1993*, International Energy Association, 1994c, p.25)

One Russian expert, requesting that he not be identified, laughed and said:
"Under the Soviet system, 30 percent theft of building materials was assumed
and taken into account before construction began. So there was enough concrete for both thieves and Ignalina [nuclear reactor]." (*New York Times*, 15
November 1992, p.3)

Unlike most areas of the globe, statistical analysis of the FSU is difficult and
often meaningless. In the first place, data are often non-existent. But also,
much of the available data are not valid, either because of accounting differences, cross-subsidization (low oil field wages but cheap housing, which is not
paid for by the Energy Ministry, for example), and even outright falsification.[21] Even correcting for these problems, the restructuring of the petroleum
sector from a government bureaucracy to an optimizing, competitive industry
(or at least strong movement in that direction), renders any analysis of the pre-
collapse data incapable of explaining current and future industry behavior.

In fact, since the collapse of the Soviet Union, data from the trade press have become increasingly available, but still suffer from a number of problems. As mentioned in the previous section, many reports give field size in terms of oil-in-place instead of proved (recoverable) reserves, many confuse total, life-of-project expenditure streams with initial capital expenditures, and so forth.

Nonetheless, analyzing the available data will provide some indication of the desirability of investment in the FSU oil sector, and future production trends.

Empirical cost estimates

Estimating actual production costs is one of the most intractable problems in petroleum economics. Few even attempt it, especially in an environment such as the FSU, where a changing policy and technical environment, combined with the data problems described above, make for a challenging task. In this section, a review of existing estimates, along with new ones by the author, is used to attempt to narrow the uncertainty.

When publications like the IEA's cited above refer to costs, it should be realized that they are, at best, rough estimates and at worst, raw guesses. In fact, the IEA used "model costs" in their estimates and noted that there had been only two estimates of Siberian production costs, both apparently based on joint ventures. They put costs at between 36 and 45 US$/metric ton, or about $5–6.5/barrel, divided evenly between capital and operating costs.

In an earlier study,[22] a number of data sets and methods were used to estimate the marginal costs of oil production in W. Siberia, and the results suggested that the costs were probably slightly below this range. Using Russian investment data, the costs seemed to be on the order of $1.5–4/barrel. Using Russian drilling data and US (North Slope Alaska) production costs, they were as high as $7/barrel. The latter number should obviously be a ceiling, since virtually all costs in Russia are lower than the comparable ones in the US.

In Table 5.8, these and other estimates of capacity costs, marginal costs, and average costs are shown.[23] The capacity costs include some historical time series, some from the sources cited, others (including *Izvestia* and Tretyakova and Heinemeier) calculated by Lynch (1990) from the investment and capacity data provided. Additionally, where capital costs necessary to maintain production have been cited, capacity costs were calculated by assuming that 10–20 percent of production needed to be replaced every year (i.e., 0.6–1.2 mb/d).

There are three groups of marginal cost estimates: two from Dienes et al. (1994), and the other one from Lynch (1990). The first from Dienes et al. is their calculation using Russian investment estimates. The second was done by what they refer to as "an unpublished 1989 study of the former oil ministry's economic research institute," applying 1990 costs to estimated necessary drilling levels. The disparity between the two is probably due to methodological and definitional differences.

Table 5.8 FSU petroleum cost estimates

Capacity costs

		$/db	
Shultz (1993)		4,000	
Izvestia (OGJ 7/3/89, p.18)	1975	966	
	1985	1,771	
	1990	2,596	
		Total	Development
US census	1966–70	988	682
(Tretyakova and	1971–75	863	597
Heinemeier, Tables 10	1976–80	1,052	803
and 11).	1981–85	2,215	1,794

Grace and Beninger (1993), idle wells

	$/db
1.2 mb/d, highest cost	4,650
0.6 mb/d, average cost	1,000

Implied capacity cost estimates from reported capital needs to maintain production.	Capital costs $bil	Assumed depletion Rate	Implied capacity cost $/db
Government estimates (OGJ 1/9/95)	2.5	10%	4,167
	3.5	20%	2,917
**other source.	7	10%	11,667
	7	20%	5,833

Marginal cost estimates
Lynch (1990)
using US cost factors

1985 W. Siberian	7.21
1985 Samotlor	6.55

Dienes et al.		1992 $/bbl
10% discount rate	1993	11.0
flat production of	1997	12.5
340 mt/yr	2000	13.2

		1990 $/bbl. Pessimist	Moderate
Russian Ministry			
economic research institute	1990	1.0	1.0
1989 study, cited in Dienes	1995	1.6	1.4
et al., pp.67–8.	2000	5.5	3.4
	2005	53.4	8.4
	2010		21.0

	1975	1980	1985	1986
Sagers		7		
Gustafson				14
Izvestia	0.69		1.26	
Gustafson (aggregate data)	0.62	1.25	4.32	
Lynch (N. Slope factor costs)	1.89	4.25	7.21	

Average costs
Dienes et al., pp.72–3.

$1990/ton		
	1987	0.3
	1992	1.1
	1995	1.7
production at 380 mt	2000	4.2
production at 450 mt	2000	15.8

Sources: Sagers, Gustafson, Izvestia, Census Bureau, from Lynch (1990). Others as noted.

The third group of marginal cost estimates includes two specific reports (Sagers and Gustafson) of unknown methodology, two calculated using the investment data given in Gustafson (1990) and an *Izvestia* report, and an estimate of what Siberian and Samotlor oil production would cost if the factor prices (i.e., labor, drilling costs, etc.) were identical to the North Slope of Alaska.

While the reliability of these estimates is not high, the clear indication is of a low-cost resource base. Capacity costs in the US and the North Sea are in the order of $10,000/db, above all but one estimate in Table 5.8, and historical marginal costs are all below world price levels, and usually well below. Even if transportation costs will be as much as $1–2/bbl, high by world standards, there remain very significant rents to be earned.

Finally, Table 5.9 lists a number of projects, mostly foreign joint ventures, where data on costs, field size, and production are available. (Several illustrative non-FSU projects are also shown for comparison.) Using the methods developed by Adelman,[24] capacity and per barrel costs are calculated. Note that in a number of cases a range of investments were provided, and each number is calculated separately. Also, some of the reports, such as for the 67 offshore fields in Kazakhstan, are so general as to be unreliable, and in other cases, particularly Sakhalin, ancillary developments such as for gas pipelines and local, non-project related infrastructure like hospitals, are included in the total. In a few cases, notably Karachaganak, there is a substantial amount of natural gas produced, but any resulting revenues are ignored here. Including them would bring down per-barrel oil costs, but not by very much.

Despite these uncertainties, it is notable that many developments came in very cheaply, at capacity costs of $2–4,000/daily barrel (compared to US costs on the order of $10,000/db) or $2–6/bbl wellhead cost, which is a fraction of world price. This suggests that the costs of new field development in the FSU are a fraction of US or even UK costs. Only in a few instances, particularly when the highest range of estimated capital expenditures is used, do projects appear uneconomic, ignoring taxes and other externalities.

Other evidence

There are other indicators that are suggestive of FSU oil economics. First and foremost is the desirability of the FSU as a petroleum province, as evidenced by the attempts by foreign oil companies to invest there despite the many political and policy uncertainties. As much as $50–70 billion (or $7–8 billion/year) in foreign investment is said to be awaiting passage of petroleum legislation.[25]

Table 5.9 FSU petroleum cost estimates

Field/ project	Primary foreign company	Development investment $mil	Field size	Peak production tb/d	Costs		
					Capacity $db	In-ground reserve $/bbl	Wellhead $/bbl
a. Russia							
Timan-Pechora	Texaco	2,000	2,400	230	8,690	$0.83	$5.60
	high est.	3,000	2,400	230	13,036	$1.25	$8.39
four fields	Fracmaster	30		14	2,143		
Neocomanian	Bechtel	250	306	22	11,364	$0.82	$7.04
Volgodeminoil	Deminex	6,500		730	8,904		
Sutormin	Texaco	80		30	2,667		
Salym	Shell	300	1,500			$0.20	
Verkhnechonskoy	Rusia Petro	575	4,500	200	2,875	$0.13	$1.70
b. Russian Far East							
Piltun-Astokhskoye		2,000	550	120	16,667	$3.64	$12.77
high est.		4,000	550	120	33,333	$7.27	$25.54
		500	600	120	4,167	$0.83	$3.12
		1,500	600	120	12,500	$2.50	$9.35
Sakhalin II	MMMMS	2,000	730	200	10,000	$2.74	$8.22
		3,000	730	200	15,000	$4.11	$12.33
c. Azerbaijan							
Azeri/Chiraq/Guneshli		8,000	4,500	700	11,429	$1.78	$8.04
Azeri/Chiraq/Guneshli		7,400	3,500			$2.11	
Azeri/Chiraq/Guneshli		7,000	3,000	600	11,667	$2.33	$8.73
d. Kazakhstan							
Karachaganak	BGC/Agip	100		60	1,667		
Karachaganak	IBGC/Agip	320	1,900	70	4,571	$0.17	$2.67
Karachaganak	BGC/Agip	3,000	1,900	2,640	1,136	$1.58	$2.20
Tengiz to date		500	4,500	130	3,846	$0.11	$2.22
Tengiz Phase I	Chevron	1,500	4,500	300	5,000	$0.33	$3.07
Tenge		370	375	36	10,278	$0.99	$6.62
Tenge		370	600	36	10,278	$0.62	$6.25
67 Offshore fields		16,500	3,000	840	19,643	$5.50	$16.26
e. Uzbekistan							
Kokdumalak	M.W. Kellog	200	1,000	90	2,222	$0.20	$1.42
OPEC fields							
Sirri A/E	Offered	600		120	5,000		
Shayba	Aramco	2,500	6,000	500	5,000	$0.42	$3.16

Notes: 20% discount rate assumed.

For Piltun-Astokskoye and Sakhalin, it was necessary to make assumptions about share of capital intended for gas and LNG projects.

For Timan-Pechora from RPI, a total investment stream was given; initial capital expenditures were calculated by assuming annual operating expenditures will equal 5% of initial capital costs.

Per barrel costs according to Adelman methodology, described in Adelman and Lynch (1986), Appendix B. All data from trade press.

The IEA's data on financial flows in the Russian oil industry (Table 5.10) are suggestive. Compared to the US and the UK, it can be seen that a far greater proportion of the Russian oil industry's revenues goes to taxes. (Note that Russian revenues for oil sold at domestic prices are less than taxes and costs combined, suggesting losses, on average, for the industry. This reflects the fact that most oil at that time was sold at domestic oil prices of one quarter the world average.) The ability of the Russians to tax at the 60 percent level and still attract investment, albeit grudgingly in some cases, implies that costs · must be a much smaller fraction of price in Russia than in the US or UK.

Table 5.10 Financial flows in the oil industry

a. billion $US	Russia	US	UK
Taxes	7.0	2.2	3.8
Costs	6.7	38.2	13.1
Revenues	11.9	46.0	25.4
b. Share of revenues (%)			
Taxes	58.8	4.8	15.1
Costs	56.3	83.0	51.6

Sources: Russia from *Russian Energy Prices, Taxes, and Costs*, IEA, 1994c, Table 1.
US from DOE, *Performance Profiles*, 1993.
UK from Dept. of Trade and Industry, *The Energy Report, Oil and Gas Resources of the United Kingdom*, vol. 2.
(1 UK pound converted to $1.6).
Costs in US and UK are expenditures.
Russian costs are approximate.

Cost trends

While the absolute level of the marginal cost of production is an important indicator of future industry behavior, for the longer term, the *change* in costs, both the rate and direction, is crucial. High stable costs might be preferable to low, rapidly rising costs depending on discount rates, tax structure, and other variables.

But the primary concern stems from the experience of the late 1980s, when marginal costs were rising rapidly, as well productivity declined due to water encroachment and returns to drilling (e.g., barrels found per exploratory well) fell due to depletion of the "mature" resource base. Increases on the order of 5 to 15 percent per year were described by many observers (see Table 5.11) as evidence that the industry was either going to face collapse and/or would need massive infusions of capital.

However, as in much of the world's oil industry, it seems likely that these cost trends were caused not by underlying physical factors, but by transient, often policy-related, effects. Outside the FSU, numerous reports of cost-cutting have shown that depletion is not the only affecting costs. As Lynch (1995c) describes, a lot of past research has incorrectly ascribed the rising cost trends of the 1980s to depletion, instead of rising factor costs and falling productivity due to rapid increases in drilling. From 1982 to 1991, the major drilling factor cost categories in the US dropped by 5.5 percent per year.

Table 5.11 Cost escalation in Soviet oil production

		Annual rate of change during period:			
	1966–70	1971–75	1976–80	1981–85	1970–85
a. Component factors (%)					
Increase in drilling costs	5.37	6.03	5.40		
Decline in new well flow rate					
USSR			9.01	7.89	
W. Siberia			17.57	11.16	
Tiumen' (fields developed pre-1971)			18.55		
Decline in new well flow rate (Shultz)					6.8
Increase in well costs					8.7
b. Average costs (%)		4.19	9.94	13.20	
c. Marginal costs (%)					
Izvestia				6.25(a)	
Tretyakova and Heinemeier		–2.66	4.04	16.05	
Using North Slope costs:					
W. Siberia			17.59	11.15	
Samotlor			18.53	11.98	

	1972–75	1976–80	1981–84
From aggregate investment data:			
Capacity (%)	–5.13	12.73	18.95
Per barrel (%)	–3.21	15.05	19.28

Sources: Drilling costs from Tretyakova and Heinemeier, p.60. New well flow rate from Gustafson, 1990, pp.91, 96. Well costs from Shultz (1993) for entire period. Average costs from Tretyakova and Heinemeier, p.8. Excludes geology fee.
Izvestia story is cited in *Oil and Gas Journal,* 3 July 1989, p.18. Marginal costs from Tretyakova and Heinemeier, pp.36, 39, but note that the annual change from 1986–90 is projected.
Note: a) Represents 1976–85, not 1981–85.

What are the likely future trends? There are positive and negative pressures. On the positive side, repair and replacement of equipment such as untreated pipe will add to costs in the short term, as will stricter environment regulations, including remediation of existing sites. But there are three reasons to anticipate that the next few years will see a substantial reversal of the rising cost trends of the 1980s in the FSU oil industry. First, the industry had undertaken a crash program in the 1980s to raise short-term production, at the expense of long-term recovery. As a result, much of the evidence shown in Table 5.11 reflects bad management, not geophysical decline. This is important because the former is a transient effect, the latter an enduring trend. Second, the Soviet economic and planning system generally resulted in losses and inefficiencies, even more so than the typical bureaucratic or state-owned operation. Observers such as the one quoted above have referred to material budgets which were overstated to allow for theft, for example. Third, as described above, the application of Western technology and management practices has already resulted in doubling of well productivity in some cases. Privatization seems certain to increase this tendency.

Overall, then, the trend in costs is likely to be negative, possibly for the next decade or more. While this might seem unlikely due to geophysical decline, i.e., the move to smaller fields in more remote locations, similar trends have been seen in other producing areas despite analysts' forecasts of rising costs.

Conclusion

Costs are not everything, but they are a very big thing. Large fields and low costs are not the only ingredient to attract foreign investment and/or expand production, but they are a necessary one. The data reviewed here confirm the economic attractiveness of the FSU's upstream sector. The fact that so many multinational oil companies are seeking investments in the FSU despite the political and regulatory turmoil substantiates what the data suggest.

And the fact that FSU costs appear to be much lower than those in many other parts of the world indicates that the economic rents from oil production are enormous. Governments have very significant incentives to allow if not encourage oil production and exports, and companies have a strong motivation to operate there. This explains why there is so much conflict over these projects, but also indicates the incentives for the parties to settle those disagreements.

Demand in the FSU

Predicting future demand is even more problematic than forecasting production. Past demand forecasting has been practically nonexistent, with Wilson (1983) the prime exception, and even he primarily extrapolated trends, as Figure 5.6 shows. His forecast proved remarkably accurate until the economic collapse occurred.

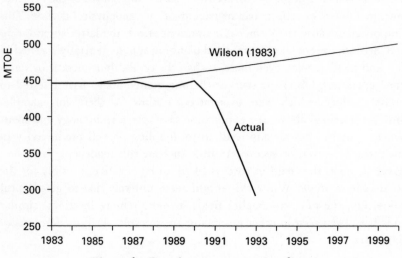

Fig. 5.6 Petroleum consumption forecast

Future FSU oil demand will be driven primarily by the conflicting pressures between improved energy efficiency and economic growth rates. Neither is easy to predict ordinarily, and especially so in economies in the early stages of structural transformation. Uncertainties include the degree of economic reform, the rate of economic growth, the level of domestic prices, and the role of energy-intensive heavy industries. Add to that the possibility that nuclear and coal might be de-emphasized, though probably in favor of gas rather than oil, and that the uncertainty about energy demand is compounded by fuel mix uncertainties.

The poor level of energy efficiency in the FSU is well known. Centralized planning and a lack of price signals have, logically, made consumers wasteful. For example, apartment tenants pay a flat (and very low) fee for their gas supplies, and modify temperatures in the winter by opening windows.[26] Dienes et al. have estimated that energy consumption in the FSU appears to be 58 percent above the level for a market economy with its economic and geographical configuration, implying wastage of 500 MTOE (or 10 mb/d oil equivalent) in 1990.[27]

How quickly the FSU economy might move towards "efficient" use of energy is, of course, impossible to predict. However, assuming that the capital stock undergoes relatively rapid replacement, it seems reasonable to anticipate that FSU energy efficiency might reach OECD levels over the next two decades. In that case, the underlying implication is that there would be a 2–2.5 percent exogenous energy efficiency improvement per year, above and beyond the typical energy efficiency improvements due to technological advances.

The other factor determining energy consumption is, as mentioned, economic growth. The prospect of rapid economic growth (what Yergin and Gustafson refer to as *Chudo*) cannot be discounted, although as with oil production, the prospects do not appear to be imminent. Dienes et al. (1994) see 5 percent per year as possible, particularly after the advent of market reforms (the timing of which varies by scenario). And in recent IEW surveys, although most respondents see the economy declining from 1990 to 2000, the mean growth from 2000 to 2020 is 4.2 percent per year.

Thus, while moderately strong long-term economic growth on the order of 4–5 percent per year is a distinct possibility, continued efficiency improvements will almost certainly keep energy demand growth much closer to OECD levels of 1.5 percent per year rather than the 4–5 percent per year typical in developing countries. In all likelihood, oil demand will grow about 2 percent per year over the next decade or so. This would add about 1 mb/d to current demand by 2005, and would have only a small impact on the amount of oil available for export.

Natural Gas

Russian gas remains an important part of the FSU energy sector, but it is being considered here primarily for its impact on the petroleum industry in the FSU and worldwide. Even without extensive analysis, certain developments seem likely given what is known about the economics of production and transportation.

Russian gas exports to W. Europe continue to grow and remain quite profitable overall, but are constrained by a lack of sales opportunities and, to some degree, by infrastructure problems, including the difficulties involving the transit through the Ukraine.[28] Cost estimates made by outside observers have repeatedly come in well below delivered prices to W. Europe, typically in the range of $2.00–2.50/Mcf, versus prices on the order of $3.50/Mcf, as shown in Table 5.12. Given a number of undeveloped supergiant fields in W. Siberia, and the fact that pipeline costs, unlike mineral resources, tend to decline over time, it seems clear that no major increase in the cost of delivering natural gas is likely for the next decade or two.[29]

The possibility exists, therefore, that discounted Russian gas to W. Europe will result in a significant displacement of oil use in power generation, refineries, and heavy industry. This would tend to offset the positive effect of weak oil prices, keeping European oil demand relatively depressed, but the impact will probably be delayed to the point where it is blunted, with the possible exception of the effect on fuel oil markets and crude price differentials.

Construction of a pipeline from Turkmenistan to W. Europe or E. Asia could prove more important. However, the distances are so long and costs so great that it is highly unlikely to get under way in the coming decade. Iran has been unable for two decades to find a viable route for long-distance export of natural gas except through the Russian pipeline system, displacing Russian gas west into Europe. Here, the previous caveats about gas demand apply.

Table 5.12   FSU delivered natural gas costs to Western Europe

Description	Cost ($/Mcf)	Notes
Urengoi to W. Germany	$2.00	Marginal cost
For non-FSU	$0.77	Current costs
To Russian border	$2.00–2.20	Costs for new pipelines
From Barents	$3.00–4.00	From offshore fields
Estimates by Birman of costs to border:		
Scenario	($/Mcf)	Time period
Actual	$0.35	Actual costs in 1992
Actual	$0.73	Actual costs in 1995
Delivery level of: 790	$0.93	Projected for 2000
Delivery level of: 852	$1.17	Projected for 2000
Delivery level of: 1,000	$3.28	Projected for 2000

Sources: Adelman and Lynch (1986); IEA 1993, p.58; Arthur D. Little estimates. Cited in Dienes et al., p.77.

In Asia, the possibility of significantly greater FSU gas exports are quite real, and the suggestion of the oil company Sidanko, that 30 bcm/yr (1 tcf) could be exported to China should be taken quite seriously. As Table 5.13 shows, it should be possible to deliver natural gas from E. Siberian fields to Beijing for about $1.61/Mcf, to S. Korea for $1.50–2.00/Mcf, and landed in

Japan for $1.90–2.30/Mcf, particularly if a phased project is used with looping of pipelines. (Note that transit fees, taxes, and royalties are not included in these estimates.)

Table 5.13   Cost of pipeline gas, E. Siberia to Osaka

Basic costs	Distance (Km)	Cost per 100 Kms ($/Mcf)	Total cost
Production costs			$0.25
Transportation costs			
Irkutsk–Harbin	2,000	$0.05	$1.00
Harbin–Beijing	1,200	$0.03	$0.36
Harbin–Seoul (via N. Korea)	1,000	$0.03	$0.30
Harbin–Luda	900	$0.03	$0.27
Harbin–Seoul (subsea)	500	$0.10	$0.50
Seoul–Ulsan	250	$0.03	$0.08
Ulsan–Honshu (subsea)	200	$0.10	$0.20
Land point to Osaka	400	$0.08	$0.32

Project costs (simple) Route	Cost $/Mcf
Irkutsk–Beijing	$1.61
Irkutsk–Seoul (land route)	$1.55
Irkutsk–Seoul (subsea)	$2.02
Irkutsk–Osaka (via N. Korea)	$2.15
Irkutsk–Osaka (via Luda)	$2.62

All transportation costs assumed constant;
segment costs are added.

Project costs (looped) Route	Cost $/Mcf
Irkutsk–Beijing	$1.61
Irkutsk–Seoul (land route)	$1.35
Irkutsk–Seoul (subsea)	$1.82
Irkutsk–Osaka (via N. Korea)	$1.89
Irkutsk–Osaka (via Luda)	$2.26

Note: Costs estimated assuming that previous segments are looped (i.e., to Harbin, Seoul), and that looping costs are 80% of original costs.

Given that China has the world's largest population, an economic growth in double digits, and currently gets 75 percent of its energy from coal, the potential market for gas is huge. It could absorb all initial gas volumes for some time to come, primarily displacing coal use in homes and industry.[30] Once the network is extended to S. Korea and Japan, there is greater potential to displace oil use in the industrial sector. However, a pipeline is unlikely to reach Korea or Japan before the middle of the next decade.

LNG from Sakhalin faces a different set of problems, namely high costs. Although the Sakhalin I and II projects appear ready to move forward, and while they nominally include LNG projects, the costs for delivered LNG are so high (about 50 percent above current prices, according to Toichi, 1994) as to make the projects undesirable. More likely, the oil fields will be developed and the gas delayed, as allowed for in the contracts.

The Near-term Future

Unquestionably, the FSU suffers from many short-term problems, including lack of petroleum legislation, inconstant and exorbitant taxation, political instability, and jurisdictional conflicts over rents, ownership, and investment. There is also no doubt that large-scale developments like field developments off Sakhalin or a Kazakhi export pipeline will, once commenced, require a significant amount of time to be completed.

However, a sharp rise in FSU oil exports in the next two years is not out of the question. Although few, if any, analysts foresee such an event, recall that the Kuwait oil fires were widely predicted to require 3–5 years *merely to extinguish*, whereas production was restored in less than two years. And the North Sea, which is the most closely monitored producing province in the world, has two years in a row surprised the industry by showing sharp increases.

Could the FSU similarly surprise observers? Yes, though not necessarily easily. Most oil analysts are preoccupied with repeatedly delayed foreign investments, and the proposed mega-projects, while ignoring smaller developments such as the return of idle wells to production. The fixation on the need for outside assistance ignores the fact that the Soviet oil industry at one time led the world, producing a record 12.6 mb/d in 1987 without foreign capital and with minimal foreign technology.

The possibility that production will begin to increase as a result of the domestic industry's efforts seems increasingly likely. Considering monthly data (which are admittedly somewhat unreliable), the year-on-year decline seems to be diminishing and perhaps reversing (Figure 5.7). Also, there have been reports of the Russian oil industry equipment producers' business picking up, which not only is bullish for production, but suggests that many of the problems caused by the political and organizational turmoil from the Soviet Union's collapse are finally easing.[31]

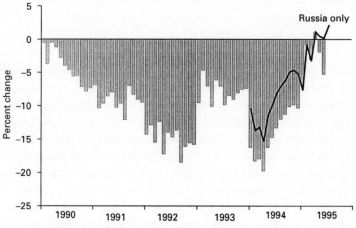

Fig. 5.7   FSU production: change from previous year

One indicator is the change in the reason for the tens of thousands of idle wells, as the two following quotes illustrate.

> During the last two years, oil and gas production enterprises have been subject to consistent shortages in supply of material and technical resources needed to keep wells producing . . . The number of idle wells has, therefore, increased sharply. As of Mar. 1, 1992, there were more than 25,000 idle wells . . . 17.3 percent of total. (*Oil and Gas Journal,* 2 August 1993, p.44).

> The shortage of solvent buyers either at home or in neighboring republics makes it likely that the flow of crude to the West will hold at around last year's 1.6 million barrels a day level through 1994 . . . Indeed, the inability of refiners to pay for and sell products has forced the closure of some 238,000 b/d of capacity from over 5,800 wells, according to the Russian Oil Bulletin. As a result, exports may first go up, not down (*Petroleum Intelligence Weekly,* 9 May 1994, p.2).

Whereas the lack of drilling capital for workovers, insufficient spare parts, etc., prevented many wells from being produced in the early 1990s, recently it has been the lack of markets which has held this oil off the market. This problem should be alleviated in the near future, as plans to expand the now-underutilized Druzhba oil pipeline from Eastern to Western Europe, other pipelines and new port facilities could add 1.2 to 2.25 mb/d of export capacity per year.[32] Obviously, all of this would not be added at once, and upstream capacity could not fill it quickly even if it was, but it seems likely that the next 1–2 years will see improvements in export capacity, higher exports, and more cash to the industry, which can then invest in more production and export capacity.

The Policy Environment

There remain numerous aspects of the policy environment in the FSU which are creating problems for the petroleum industry, not least of which is the upcoming presidential election. At this writing, it appears as if Boris Yeltsin will win the election over Gennady Zyuganov. However, for the past year many observers saw a strong likelihood that Zyuganov would win. In such a case, his likely policies towards the oil industry, and especially foreign investment, were highly uncertain but expected to be unfavorable. He has been accused of proposing different policies to different audiences, being much more accommodating to foreign businessmen in overseas fora than when speaking to political rallies within Russia. Even if he knows what he intends to do after the election, he may alter those plans once in office.

Similarly, Yeltsin seems to intend to continue the process of reform if reelected, especially if he makes deals with the third and fourth place candidates in the run-off (Lebed and Yavlinksy). But his own economic policies have been less than stable during his first term, and just precisely how he would deal with, for example, reform of the oil pipeline system is not clear.

In terms of legislation, foreign investors want a strong, unambiguous law which authorizes production-sharing agreements. However, the industry has expressed strong concerns about the legislation which was passed last year, particularly seeking clarification regarding provisions in the law concerning arbitration, grandfathering, custom duties exemptions, export rights, etc. The law originally passed by the Duma met with strong approval by the foreign multinationals, but it was then modified following opposition about the lack of parliamentary involvement in contracts, the provision of exemptions to investors that appeared to conflict with Russian law, and so forth (Pugliaresi and Hensel, 1996).

On the other hand, the recent signing of contracts to develop Sakhalin reserves by two different groups indicates that either the legislation is acceptable or that the consortia have confidence that the refinements they seek will be made. Also, the apparent triumph of the reformers in the presidential election has assuaged many foreign investors' concerns.

Taxation is another area of great concern to the industry, foreign and domestic companies alike. The government has sought to maximize its tax revenues from the petroleum industry (with the encouragement of the OECD), without raising taxes so high as to prevent investment and/or production. However, the generally chaotic fiscal and regulatory system in Russia has left oil companies facing a variety of demands for funds, including restrictions on currency exchange, pipeline tariffs, and tariffs on imported equipment. One particularly insidious approach has been to agree to rescind a tax, often just after it is applied, but to force companies to make the payments first and apply for a refund, which is usually much delayed. Aside from the straight financial cost of these tactics, the uncertainty about future tax levels has a negative impact on the apparent value of investing in Russia.

A recent assessment of the tax bill on the industry concluded that 46 percent of revenues went to taxes in 1995, up from 41 percent in 1994.[33] Aside from being relatively high, the nature of the taxes has a deleterious effect on investment. Because they tax revenues rather than profits they are regressive, rather than progressive, and the impact on investment in fields with high costs is negative. Again, however, the current political situation suggests that many of the problems will be fixed and the fiscal regime will become stable.

Finally, what is referred to as pipeline politics remains a problem, although this difficulty, too, appears moving towards resolution. In Russia proper, the monopoly of the state-owned Transneft has created many problems. Some foreign companies apparently feel that they are not giving adequate priority to existing pipeline capacity, and attempts to build new capacity, such as at Timan Pechora, run into resistance from Transneft. In the southern republics, notably Azerbaijan and Kazakhstan, efforts to develop new routes that would be independent of Russian control have been stymied. The United States does not want pipelines going through Iran, Turkey wants pipelines to the Mediterranean not the Black Sea, Russia wants pipelines to pass through its territory, etc.

However, signs of resolution are appearing in part as Transneft yields some control over new projects, while accepting the role of operator and/or partner. There are preliminary agreements to export larger volumes of oil from the southern republics, with the initial amounts moving through rehabilitated Russian pipelines. There are signs that a new pipeline from the Timan Pechora area will finally be constructed, allowing some of the foreign joint ventures to proceed.[34] Overall, it appears as if progress continues to be made in improving the existing system, as well as in reaching agreement on new, large-scale export pipelines.

Although some companies remain extremely reluctant to commit to large-scale investments in the FSU until more of these problems have actually been resolved, others appear ready to go ahead. It is important for the analyst to

remember that political risk is the mother's milk of the upstream oil industry. Companies have explored for, developed, and produced oil through
coups, revolutions, and civil wars, to say nothing of price controls and exorbitant taxation. One would do well to recall the recent story on the industry,
where the following observation was made: "When asked recently to identify
the riskiest place in the world to invest in exploration, the boss of one large
American company snapped 'California'."[35]

Conclusions

Many possible scenarios can be drawn from the above, but it is important to
consider the difference between the transient and mutable factors, like taxes
and investment policies, and the physical, less variable elements, like
resource abundance and costs. The large, low-cost nature of the FSU's oil
resource suggests that it will be an increasingly large exporter, perhaps
rivaling the larger OPEC countries. While the FSU might have little incremental impact on the oil market for the mid-term future (3–5 years), the possibility of a rapid turnaround, adding as much as 2 mb/d in as little as two
years, exists.

For oil production (and exports) to remain depressed, the following must
happen:

— petroleum legislation remains unsigned for years;
— taxes remain so high as to prevent investment;
— cost trends from the days of the collapse prove to be geophysical, rather
  than managerial; and
— the organizational problems from the collapse of the Soviet Union remain
  unresolved.

Given that these problems are all transient or policy-related, it seems difficult to assume their indefinite persistence. If, as reported, there is as much as
$7–8 billion per year in foreign investment waiting for passage of petroleum
legislation, assuming that half will go to upstream developments at
$8,000/db (a conservative estimate), then 500 tb/d/yr in production could be
added. Since domestic companies seem to have largely stabilized production
without foreign assistance, that amount would represent incremental exports,
minus perhaps 100 tb/d/yr growth in consumption. Annual export growth
on the order of 200–400 tb/d would not be a dominant factor in the world
oil market, where demand is growing by 1–1.5 mb/d/yr, but it would be a
contributing factor to weak long-term prices.

Of course, the size of oil exports is not the only factor which will affect the
world oil market. Increased use of Siberian gas in the FSU and Eastern and

Western Europe, China, and possibly East and South Asia would release large amounts of residual fuel oil on the market. This would be partly offset by refinery upgrading in the FSU. Differentials between light and heavy crudes will probably be more volatile as a result, depending on the timing of the conflicting developments.[36]

The restructuring of the FSU's oil industry into a group of private, integrated oil companies should not only improve both the efficiency of operations, but make them more predictable. The companies should behave more as profit-maximizing organizations, resulting in much greater transparency in the FSU market and reducing uncertainty about the volatility of oil exports, which have had a destabilizing effect on the market in the past.

Of course, the most optimal effect would be if the increased revenues made a difference for the FSU economies. If the optimistic levels of oil exports are reached, they will add as much as $25 billion in foreign exchange, and perhaps half or more of that in government revenue.

Still, it is important to recognize that oil revenues by themselves will not solve the FSU's economic problems. A visit to other producers, whether Nigeria or Louisiana, will demonstrate that. However, the preferred example is Meiji Japan, which, a century ago, used the country's natural resources (such as coal) to gain the capital necessary to industrialize.[37] Oil money will not solve the problem, but oil money *used wisely* can take the FSU a major step down the road from socialism to capitalism.

CHAPTER 6

Forecasting the Demand for Gasoline in the GCC Countries

Abdul-Razak Faris Al-Faris

Introduction

The demand for gasoline in the Gulf oil-producing countries has increased considerably during the last two decades. This rapid growth is the result of growth in income, population, migration, urbanization, and stock of vehicles.

In recent years, the GCC countries have become increasingly concerned with the implications of this accelerating increase in domestic energy consumption. For some of these countries, growth in internal demand reduces oil export availability. Within these countries, concern for the environment is also growing and already having a major impact on policies in many areas. The scope of this concern is broad and includes air pollution and urban congestion.

The need for the government to take responsibility for a detailed long-term view of energy balance has increased. Fears about future scarcity and the need to establish priorities for GCC development have extended the time horizons of energy policy, and necessitated an energy demand forecast.

Projections of energy demand are also important on other grounds. They play a crucial role in determining the necessary mix of products to be refined at any given period, and in planning future refining technology and capacity. Further changes in the patterns of domestic energy demand may require a process of restructuring the refining industry and substantial programs of investment. Energy projections, moreover, will help to monitor the general development and direction of the energy market in the GCC countries, for example, as a background against which to view the potential future role of non-energy sources in the economy, and the prospects for energy efficiency especially in the transportation sector.

The purpose of this chapter is to estimate future gasoline consumption in the GCC countries into the year 2010, and its implications for energy policies.

The projection is based on a formal statistical model allowing for various scenarios of energy prices and economic development. The chapter provides a summary background of gasoline consumption and prices in these countries over the last two decades; describes the equation which forms the basis for statistical analysis and future forecasting; presents and discusses the main results; and sets out the major conclusions and policy implications.

Background

The GCC countries occupy a major role in the global energy picture, particularly in the international crude oil market. In 1993, these countries accounted for 22 percent of total world crude oil production, and an even higher share − 36.2 percent − of total world exports. They possess over 46 percent of the world's proven petroleum reserves (see the BP *Statistical Review of World Energy 1994*).

In 1970, the present six members of the Gulf Cooperation Council together consumed around 66.7 thousand b/d of crude oil and refined products, which constituted an average of 0.8 percent of their production. More than twenty years later, in 1993, the picture had been transformed. The combined demand of these states increased to 1.3 million b/d, or 8.7 percent of their output (Table 6.1) between 1970 and 1993. Total GCC petroleum consumption between 1970 and 1980 grew at an annual rate of 28 percent, a rate which surpassed the growth rates of the GDP, total capital formation, and GDP per capita. The steady erosion of these countries' export earnings since the early 1980s, due to unfavorable conditions in the oil market and accelerated depreciation in United States dollar exchange rates, caused a marked slowdown in the GCC's economies. Subsequently, oil consumption growth rates declined to an annual average of 3.7 percent between the years 1980 and 1993.

Table 6.1   Oil production and consumption in the GCC countries (thousand b/d)

	Saudi	UAE	Kuwait	Oman	Qatar	Bahrain
1970						
Output	3,600	780	2,990	294	362	77
Consumption	42.5	2.2	14.1	1.8	1.9	4.2
%	1.1	0.3	0.5	0.6	0.5	5.5
1980						
Output	9,900	1,712	1,663	283	473	48
Consumption	581	98.8	69.1	13.2	9.7	16.3
%	5.8	5.8	4.2	4.7	2.1	34
1993						
Output	8,695	2,435	1,950	780	500	42
Consumption	908	169	92	55	16	18
%	10.4	6.9	4.7	7.0	3.2	42.9

Sources: IEA, *Energy Statistics and Balances of non-OECD Countries 1990–1991*, Paris, 1993, and BP, *Statistical Review of World Energy*, June 1994.

Gasoline consumption in the GCC countries has increased more than tenfold over the period 1970–91. This rapid growth has been to a great extent underpinned by accelerating growth in crude oil production as well as by a process of urbanization. In the early 1970s, gasoline accounted for an average of 33.1 percent of total final oil consumption, and its share dropped to 26.8 percent in 1991.

Rapid structural changes in domestic economies during the second half of the 1970s and the early 1980s boosted the demand for fuel – especially in the industrial sector, electricity generation, and desalination. The share of gasoline during this period subsequently dropped to an average of one quarter. Economic slowdown and widespread substitution of natural gas for heavy fuel reversed this trend and gave gasoline a greater fraction of total oil consumption during the second half of the 1980s (Table 6.2).

Table 6.2   Percentage share of gasoline in total oil consumption in the GCC countries

Year	Saudi	UAE	Kuwait	Oman	Qatar	Bahrain
1970	27.3	36.4	51.8	24.4	42.0	16.7
1975	22.8	19.6	45.6	29.9	29.6	13.6
1980	15.0	13.8	30.3	34.6	40.2	16.0
1985	18.0	18.2	22.9	35.8	44.3	25.2
1990	15.9	15.2	20.0	38.2	44.5	27.5
1991	15.9	15.2	15.7	38.2	48.9	26.6

Sources: OAPEC, *Annual Report of the Secretary General*, Various Issues, and IEA, *Energy Statistics and Balances of non-OECD Countries 1990-1991*, Paris, 1993.

Disparity in gasoline share in the Gulf countries is only an indication of the group's different states of economic development, endowment of energy resources, and the level of GDP per capita. The wide variation in the levels of gasoline demand is also caused by sharp differences in energy prices paid by consumers. As Table 6.3 and Figure 6.1 show, there have been wide differences in transport fuel prices in these countries. Gasoline prices in Saudi Arabia were less than 40 percent of their counterparts in Bahrain and Oman in the early 1970s. After the first oil price adjustment in 1973, domestic gasoline prices were further reduced in Saudi Arabia and Kuwait, and maintained at their prevailing nominal levels or raised slightly in other member states. During the 1980s, Saudi's gasoline prices were about one quarter of those in Oman and Bahrain.

Another characteristic of gasoline prices in the GCC countries is the nominal rigidity. In all these states, pump prices have been regulated by government, and national oil companies, which control domestic distribution, and set their prices according to certain guidelines. In all the Gulf countries, there is a high degree of industry concentration, and product price differentials are minimal or non-existent. Gasoline prices (and until recently, energy prices in general) have not been facilitated as a policy instrument in the domestic economy. For a variety of reasons, governments have been reluctant to pass on fluctuations in international crude prices to consumers. As a result, internal energy prices have risen markedly less than world prices and less than increases in other developing nations.[1]

Table 6.3   Nominal gasoline prices in the GCC countries (US $/barrel)

Year	Saudi	UAE	Kuwait	Oman	Qatar	Bahrain
1970	7.96	9.90	8.91	18.14	8.18	20.0
1971	9.21	9.93	9.93	18.19	8.21	21.94
1972	10.55	10.75	10.15	19.69	8.89	20.26
1973	10.11	11.79	12.06	21.55	9.75	18.46
1974	8.73	15.46	12.21	25.11	9.87	18.27
1975	5.77	17.44	11.41	25.11	9.91	18.87
1976	5.57	15.26	10.88	27.87	9.83	18.87
1977	5.47	15.46	11.10	25.57	9.84	21.56
1978	9.27	15.59	11.56	25.57	11.89	30.62
1979	10.59	17.88	11.51	32.71	12.22	30.20
1980	10.10	25.48	11.77	51.13	12.61	29.94
1981	10.20	25.73	11.41	56.20	12.67	34.38
1982	9.34	30.18	20.80	54.59	12.67	41.48
1983	8.78	40.93	24.55	52.98	20.82	46.71
1984	12.39	44.78	24.17	52.98	25.12	47.83
1985	13.12	44.78	23.79	52.98	25.12	47.83
1986	12.87	41.73	24.62	47.90	25.12	47.83
1987	12.90	37.14	25.68	47.59	25.12	50.22
1988	12.90	36.20	25.64	47.59	25.12	52.93
1989	13.54	36.20	24.36	47.59	25.12	53.81
1990	13.85	36.20	–	47.59	25.12	53.81

Sources: OAPEC, *Annual Report of the Secretary General*, Various Issues, and IEA, *Energy Statistics and Balances of non-OECD Countries 1990-1991*, Paris, 1993.

Modeling the Demand for Gasoline

There are many forecasting methods that can be used to predict future gasoline demand and, before proceeding, we need to discuss briefly the method chosen. Energy forecasting has relied on three primary modeling techniques:[2]

1. Subjective forecasts are based on judgment, intuition, and industry knowledge.
2. Univariate forecasts are based entirely on past observations in a given

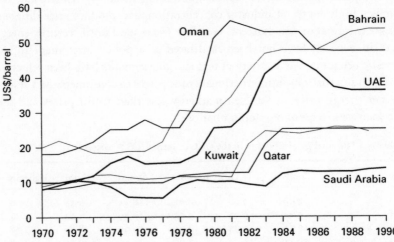

Fig. 6.1 Nominal gasoline prices in the GCC countries (US$/barrel)

time series. This is achieved by fitting a model to the given data, and then extrapolating. This method comprises a variety of models, such as the Box-Jenkins forecasting procedure (ARIMA), and the Granger and Newbold stepwise autoregression. These models suffer many shortcomings, their primary disadvantage being a "general inability to model the underlying influences on energy demand. They are not useful as policy tools, and are inaccurate when significant changes in determining variables are expected in the future."[3]

3.   Multivariate procedures start with determining the structural relationship between the relevant variables. These models include: multiple regression and simultaneous equations.

The method of forecasting in this chapter is based on the econometric model that belongs to the third category. The assumptions of the model and its main characteristics when applied to gasoline demand in the GCC countries will be summarized here.[4]

Most gasoline demand models are intimately related to the partial adjustment model proposed by Balestra and Nerlove (1966). Houthakker and Taylor (1970) tried to relax the strictly linear form of this model to an equation which is linear in logarithms. The basic assumption of the model is that consumers only partially adjust to an equilibrium demand. The adjustment is partial because of habit formation, earlier commitments, costs involved in replacing the existing capital stock, or lack of information.

The partial adjustment model consists of two equations. The first equation defines the equilibrium value, and expresses desired demand Q^*_t as a function of a vector of exogenous variables X_t as follows:

$$Q^*_t = X_t B + \xi_t \qquad (1)$$

The second states that the current value of Q_t adjusts to its equilibrium level only slowly:

$$Q_t - Q_{t-1} = (1-\delta)(Q^*_t - Q^*_{t-1}) + v_t \qquad (2)$$

Solving (1) and (2) for Q_t we have the following equation expressed in a general form:

$$Q_t = X_t B + \delta Q_{t-1} + \mu_t \qquad (3)$$

δ is the adjustment coefficient which measures the proportion by which the divergence between the equilibrium level and the actual level is bridged in period t. In the extreme case, where $\delta = 1$, the two equations (desired and actual) are equal, the adjustment is instantaneous, and we end up with a static model. The closer δ is to one, the more rapid is the adjustment to a shock to the system, and the smaller it is, the slower is the adjustment.

Equation (3) could be expressed in the following form:

$$Q_t = \zeta_0 + \zeta_1 P_t + \zeta_2 Y_t + \zeta_3 Q_{t-1} + \zeta_t \qquad (4)$$

If this equation is estimated in a logarithmic functional form, then the variables' coefficients represent the short-run income and price elasticities.

The Empirical Results

The statistical analysis of gasoline consumption is based on country-specific demand, using annual data covering the period 1970–91. The reason for not using a pooled time series is quite obvious: there exist distinct differences among the GCC countries in terms of the determinants such as GDP, domestic energy prices, etc. Gasoline refers to both premium and regular brands. Due to the fact that in the GCC countries all private cars, taxis, and light vehicles are gasoline driven, the model did not attempt to incorporate a fuel-substitution mechanism, which assumes that relative fuel prices determine the choice of refined products.

The model was estimated by using Ordinary Least Squares (OLS). The variables for each country are expressed in its own currency to eliminate the effect of exchange rate fluctuations. The dependent variable Q_t is the total gasoline consumption in each country, and Q_{t-1} is consumption in the previous year. P_t is the price of gasoline and Y_t is a measure of income, and two proxies are used: GDP and private consumption.

Estimates for equation (4) are displayed in Table 6.4 with t-test in parentheses. R2 is the coefficient of multiple determination, and DW is the Durbin-Watson statistic for serial correlation. Because this test has some defects in detecting first-order serial correlation in an autoregressive model like the one under consideration here, it was supplemented by the Lagrange multiplier (LM) test of serial correlation. Data sources and definitions are discussed in the Appendix.

The regression results indicate that all coefficients have the expected signs and most of them are significantly different from zero. The average short-run elasticity of gasoline prices in the GCC countries is found to be -0.14, with a range of estimates varying from -0.08 for UAE to -0.29 for Oman. The direct interpretation of these results is that the demand for gasoline in the Gulf countries is inelastic with respect to price in the short run. The pricing policies of the Gulf countries, which maintained domestic nominal fuel prices at an artificially low level, could be a contributory factor for the small coefficients. Moreover, as indicated by Pindyck (1979), using data where prices have changed infrequently and on a smaller range may bias the elasticity estimate downward.

Table 6.4   Empirical estimates of gasoline demand in the GCC countries

Variable	Saudi	UAE	Kuwait	Oman	Qatar	Bahrain
P	-0.09	-0.08	-0.10	-0.29	-0.14	-0.16
	(3.4)	(1.1)	(1.40)	(4.6)	(2.0)	(2.9)
Y	0.03	0.28	0.07	0.27	0.02	0.11
	(2.4)	(2.8)	(3.6)	(10.2)	(1.97)	(3.6)
Q_{t-1}	0.72	0.71	0.94	0.76	0.80	0.91
	(9.0)	(12.2)	(13.0)	(23.1)	(8.3)	41
R²	0.9981	0.9779	0.9435	0.9983	0.9976	0.9935
DW	2.3	2.7	2.1	1.4	2.1	2.4
LM	5.3	3.2	8.3	6.4	9.8	15.5

Income elasticities of demand in all cases have the correct sign, and all are significant at 5 percent. The average short-run income elasticity is 0.13, with estimates for individual countries ranging from 0.02 for Qatar to 0.28 for the UAE. Income elasticities in the GCC countries are notoriously small, and this could reflect the fact that private transportation in these countries is considered a necessity by the majority of people.

The Forecast Assumptions

In order to form a view of the possible levels of future gasoline demand, a number of assumptions need to be made. Because of the uncertainty inherent in projecting the future path of gasoline demand, our projections will not rely on a single hypothesis, but will be based instead on a set of different scenarios of growth in the economy and of domestic transport fuel prices. It should be emphasized, however, that the aim of our exercise is to identify the probable outcome of a given set of assumptions and policies. The question of whether these policies are optimal is beyond the scope of this study.

Changes in energy intensity and elasticity are a reflection of numerous underlying factors, such as the growth rates and composition of GDP, the level of activity in individual energy-using sectors, the state of technology, the price of energy, and demographic and sociological factors. In order to keep the analysis tractable, two main variables, economic growth rates and domestic gasoline prices, have been emphasized. Analysis of historic trends in transport fuel demand in the previous section shows that these two factors play a major determining role. Nevertheless, both factors are difficult to forecast because they are influenced by many internal and external forces. Accordingly, the forecasting reported here makes use of three different economic growth scenarios (high, medium, and low), and two gasoline price scenarios (high and low).

Growth in Economic Activity

One of the most important determinants of gasoline demand in the GCC countries has been the growth of economic activity. Gasoline consumption is closely linked to economic growth and any expansion of the economy requires a proportional increase in energy use. GDP is the usual measure of economic activity, but it is recognized that its value in forecasting may fluctuate through time because of a number of important effects:

1. economic growth may witness a great variation due to volatility in the world petroleum market;
2. economic growth may not entail equality in income distribution, and this

has a strong bearing on the demand for private transport and gasoline consumption;

3. the effects economic growth has on public expenditures and energy subsidies.

In our projections, three different views of the GCC economic growth in the longer term have been envisaged. The Gulf countries are divided into two groups. The first (Saudi Arabia, UAE, Kuwait, and Qatar) has vast oil and gas reserves, and good prospects for sustainable economic development. The second group (Oman and Bahrain) has limited mineral reserves, and potentially lower growth prospects.

Table 6.5 contains economic growth assumptions in these two groups, ranging from an optimistic view with annual output growth rates of 5–8 percent to a pessimistic view with growth rates of 1.5–2.5 percent.

Gasoline Prices

There are two gasoline price scenarios in our projections: high and low. As mentioned earlier, domestic gasoline prices in the GCC countries are set by the respective government, and prices do not necessarily reflect costs. Moreover, the prices are – in the majority of Gulf states – low compared with international prices. The sharp fall in the price of crude oil in 1986 raised important new questions about domestic energy pricing policies; nonetheless, these prices still have no strong connection with world energy pricing policies. Our price hypotheses are complicated by two other factors. The first is the question as to whether the GCC governments will take further steps to increase domestic energy prices to remedy a budget deficit if crude oil export revenue plunges. The second is the fact that there has been no consensus among energy analysts on the likely future trajectory of crude oil prices.[5]

Table 6.5 Economic growth assumptions: average annual rates

	High		Medium		Low	
	1992–2000	2000–2010	1992–2000	2000–2010	1992–2000	2000–2010
Group 1	5	8	3	5	2	4
Group 2	4	6	2	4	1.5	2.5

Note: Group 1: Saudi Arabia, Kuwait, UAE, and Qatar; Group 2: Oman and Bahrain.
Source: Taken from various estimates by IMF, IEA, and US Department of Energy.

For simplicity, we shall assume that for the forecast period, domestic gasoline prices will be influenced largely by budgetary needs and government policies on the environment, and not by variation in the international crude oil price. Table 6.6 displays fuel price assumptions. Both scenarios assume a constant real price of gasoline over the period 1991–95. Again, we distinguish between two groups within the GCC: the group which will have an oil-financed budget until the terminal year of our projection (2010), and the group (Oman and Bahrain), which will be obliged to achieve large savings in petroleum use. Finally, Table 6.7 shows all six scenarios and the abbreviations used to identify them in this chapter.

Table 6.6   Domestic gasoline price assumptions

	High			Low		
	1992–95	1996–2000	2000–2010	1992–95	1996–2000	2000–2010
Group 1	constant	3	5	constant	1.5	3
Group 2	constant	4	6	constant	2.5	4

Forecasting the Demand for Gasoline: 1992–2010

Forecasts are the outcome of the model specifications. Our results are no exception, and they are dependent upon the assumptions we have made. Changes in these assumptions – the future economic growth rate, energy pricing policies, environmental regulation, and dramatic changes in the international oil market, or the quota system within OPEC – will affect significantly the size of oil revenues in the Gulf countries and consequently affect domestic energy consumption.

Table 6.7   GDP growth and domestic gasoline prices: scenarios

Scenarios	Abbreviation
High GDP growth – high gasoline prices	HH
High GDP growth – low gasoline prices	HL
Medium GDP growth – high gasoline prices	MH
Medium GDP growth – low gasoline prices	ML
Low GDP growth – high gasoline prices	LH
Low GDP growth – low gasoline prices	LL

The demand projections for transport fuels for the period 1992–2010 are obtained on the basis of our primary model, equation (4), and are displayed in Tables 6.8 to 6.13. Utilizing the 1970–91 regression coefficients, the future gasoline demand is estimated by using six different scenarios. The underlying assumption of these scenarios is that variations in exogenous variables will have an impact on future fuel consumption. Several observations could be cited from these tables.

Table 6.8   Scenario one: HH

Year	Saudi	UAE	Kuwait	Oman	Qatar	Bahrain
1992	167.5	25.3	13.4	12.1	7.1	5.7
1993	173.6	26.1	15.0	12.4	7.2	6.0
1994	180.3	26.9	16.3	12.6	7.3	6.3
1995	187.3	27.7	17.7	12.9	7.4	6.7
1996	194.5	28.6	19.1	13.2	7.5	7.0
1997	201.9	29.6	20.5	13.5	7.6	7.3
1998	209.3	30.6	21.9	13.8	7.7	7.6
1999	216.9	31.6	23.5	14.2	7.8	8.0
2000	225.2	32.8	25.1	14.5	7.8	8.3
2001	234.3	34.2	27.2	14.8	7.8	8.5
2002	244.1	35.7	29.8	15.2	7.7	8.8
2003	254.5	37.3	32.8	15.5	7.6	9.0
2004	265.9	39.1	35.9	15.9	7.5	9.2
2005	277.9	40.9	39.2	16.4	7.4	9.4
2006	290.7	42.9	42.8	16.8	7.4	9.6
2007	304.4	45.0	46.7	17.2	7.2	9.7
2008	318.7	47.3	50.9	17.7	7.1	9.8
2009	334.1	49.6	55.5	18.1	7.0	9.8
2010	350.3	52.1	60.4	18.6	6.8	9.9

Table 6.9   Scenario two: HL

Year	Saudi	UAE	Kuwait	Oman	Qatar	Bahrain
1992	168.4	25.3	13.4	12.1	7.1	5.7
1993	175.5	26.1	15.0	12.4	7.2	6.0
1994	182.9	26.9	16.3	12.6	7.3	6.3
1995	190.8	27.7	17.7	12.9	7.4	6.7
1996	199.2	28.6	19.1	13.2	7.6	7.0
1997	207.8	29.6	20.5	13.5	7.7	7.4
1998	216.7	30.6	21.9	13.8	7.8	7.7
1999	226.1	31.6	23.5	14.2	7.9	8.1
2000	236.8	32.9	25.1	14.5	8.0	8.5
2001	248.5	34.3	27.2	14.8	8.0	8.9
2002	261.4	35.8	29.8	15.2	8.1	9.4
2003	275.7	37.5	32.8	15.6	8.1	9.8
2004	291.1	39.4	36.0	16.0	8.2	10.3
2005	307.9	41.3	39.6	16.4	8.2	10.7
2006	325.9	43.4	43.5	16.9	8.2	11.2
2007	345.7	45.6	47.8	17.4	8.2	11.7
2008	367.0	47.9	52.4	17.9	8.2	12.2
2009	389.8	50.5	57.3	18.3	8.2	12.7
2010	414.3	53.1	62.5	18.9	8.2	13.2

Table 6.10   Scenario three: MH

Table 6.10   Scenario three: MH

Year	Saudi	UAE	Kuwait	Oman	Qatar	Bahrain
1992	167.1	25.2	13.4	12.1	7.1	5.7
1993	172.4	25.8	15.0	12.4	7.2	6.0
1994	177.8	26.4	16.3	12.6	7.3	6.2
1995	183.4	27.0	17.5	12.8	7.4	6.5
1996	188.6	27.7	18.6	13.0	7.5	6.8
1997	193.7	28.2	19.6	13.2	7.6	7.0
1998	198.5	28.8	20.5	13.4	7.6	7.2
1999	203.2	29.4	21.4	13.6	7.6	7.4
2000	207.9	30.1	22.3	13.8	7.6	7.6
2001	212.9	30.8	23.5	13.9	7.6	7.7
2002	218.0	31.7	24.9	14.1	7.5	7.7
2003	223.1	32.5	26.5	14.3	7.4	7.7
2004	228.4	33.5	28.0	14.5	7.3	7.7
2005	233.9	34.4	29.5	14.8	7.1	7.7
2006	239.5	35.4	31.0	15.0	7.0	7.6
2007	245.2	36.5	107.0	15.2	6.8	7.5
2008	251.0	37.5	71.2	15.4	6.6	7.3
2009	257.0	38.7	56.4	15.6	6.4	7.2
2010	263.2	39.8	49.7	15.9	6.2	7.0

Table 6.11   Scenario four: ML

Year	Saudi	UAE	Kuwait	Oman	Qatar	Bahrain
1992	167.9	25.2	13.4	12.1	7.1	5.7
1993	174.1	25.8	15.0	12.4	7.2	6.0
1994	180.2	26.4	16.3	12.6	7.3	6.2
1995	186.4	27.0	17.5	12.8	7.4	6.5
1996	192.6	27.6	18.6	13.0	7.5	6.8
1997	198.6	28.2	19.6	13.2	7.6	7.1
1998	204.6	28.8	20.5	13.4	7.7	7.3
1999	210.7	29.4	21.4	13.6	7.8	7.6
2000	217.3	30.1	22.3	13.8	7.8	7.8
2001	224.3	30.9	23.5	13.9	7.9	8.0
2002	231.7	31.8	24.9	14.1	7.9	8.2
2003	239.6	32.7	26.5	14.3	7.9	8.4
2004	247.9	33.7	28.1	14.6	7.9	8.6
2005	256.5	34.7	29.7	14.8	7.8	8.8
2006	265.6	35.8	31.5	15.1	7.8	8.9
2007	275.5	36.9	109.6	15.3	7.7	9.0
2008	285.7	38.1	73.3	15.6	7.7	9.1
2009	296.3	39.3	58.2	15.9	7.6	9.2
2010	307.4	40.5	51.4	16.1	7.5	9.3

Table 6.12   Scenario five: LH

Year	Saudi	UAE	Kuwait	Oman	Qatar	Bahrain
1992	166.9	25.2	13.4	12.1	7.1	5.7
1993	171.8	25.7	15.0	12.4	7.2	6.0
1994	176.6	26.2	16.3	12.6	7.3	6.2
1995	181.4	26.7	17.4	12.8	7.4	6.5
1996	185.6	27.1	18.3	13.0	7.5	6.7
1997	189.7	27.5	19.1	13.1	7.6	6.9
1998	193.3	28.0	19.8	13.3	7.6	7.1
1999	196.6	28.4	20.4	13.4	7.6	7.3
2000	199.8	28.8	21.1	13.6	7.6	7.4
2001	203.1	29.4	21.9	13.7	7.5	7.4
2002	206.5	30.0	22.9	13.8	7.4	7.4
2003	209.7	30.6	24.0	14.0	7.3	7.4
2004	213.1	31.2	25.0	14.1	7.1	7.3
2005	216.5	31.9	26.1	14.2	7.0	7.1
2006	219.9	32.6	27.0	14.3	6.8	7.0
2007	223.3	33.3	28.0	14.4	6.6	6.8
2008	226.7	34.1	29.0	14.5	6.4	6.6
2009	230.2	34.9	30.1	14.6	6.2	6.3
2010	233.7	35.7	31.1	14.7	6.0	6.0

Table 6.13   Scenario six: LL

Year	Saudi	UAE	Kuwait	Oman	Qatar	Bahrain
1992	167.7	25.2	13.4	12.1	7.1	5.7
1993	173.4	25.7	15.0	12.4	7.2	6.0
1994	178.9	26.2	16.3	12.6	7.3	6.2
1995	184.2	26.7	17.4	12.8	7.4	6.5
1996	189.3	27.1	18.3	13.0	7.5	6.7
1997	194.1	27.5	19.1	13.1	7.6	7.0
1998	198.7	28.0	19.8	13.3	7.7	7.2
1999	203.3	28.4	20.4	13.4	7.7	7.4
2000	208.2	28.9	21.1	13.6	7.8	7.6
2001	213.4	29.5	21.9	13.7	7.8	7.8
2002	218.7	30.1	22.9	13.9	7.8	7.9
2003	224.4	30.8	24.0	14.0	7.7	8.0
2004	230.3	31.5	25.1	14.1	7.7	8.1
2005	236.5	32.2	26.3	14.3	7.6	8.1
2006	242.8	33.0	27.5	14.4	7.6	8.2
2007	249.7	33.8	28.7	14.6	7.5	8.2
2008	256.9	34.6	29.9	14.7	7.4	8.1
2009	264.2	35.4	31.1	14.8	7.3	8.1
2010	271.7	36.3	32.2	14.9	7.2	8.0

First, gasoline is used in conjunction with the automobile stock to produce transport services. An increase in income implies a rise in wages and salaries, which will boost household gasoline consumption. In addition, growth in GDP will increase the demand for vehicles for business and leisure and this will, in turn, increase the demand for fuel. As indicated earlier, income elasticities of demand for gasoline in the GCC countries are noticeably small. A contributory factor to low income elasticity is that driving comes from long-term habit formation, which means that it does not adjust quickly to variations in income. Habit formation may reflect the relatively high level of income in the Gulf states. Linked to this issue is the question of gasoline cost of incremental increase in output. The income elasticity used by the model measures the proportional change in transport fuel demand in response to a 1 percent change in GDP. There are two shortcomings with the elasticity as defined above. The first is that the estimated coefficients measure short-term and not long-term income elasticities. Second, these short-term elasticities will not necessarily have the same value in the future.

In the long run, it is expected that the demand for gasoline will tend to rise less rapidly than economic activity. This implies increases in energy efficiency as GDP grows. This partly reflects the increased efficiency of new cars, which means fuel consumption will grow more slowly than the size of the fleet, and also partly reflects the tendency of consumers to spend a smaller portion of their income on fuels as they become richer.

Second, the price elasticity of demand for transport fuel will have a significant impact on our energy requirements in the years ahead. The elasticity of gasoline prices manifests itself in several ways. The demand for gasoline rises less rapidly if fuel prices rise faster than increase in real wages. This is so because, with higher gasoline prices, transport fuel will be used more efficiently. Consumers will tend to drive less mileage and switch to cars that require less energy. One has to bear in mind that adjustments in energy demand in response to increases in fuel prices will not occur instantly. Consumers are not likely to replace or retrofit all energy-using devices as soon as they see higher energy prices. The more likely response is a gradual adaption to the changes.

Third, in all scenarios, higher prices of gasoline in real terms will work to reduce the demand for transport fuel. However, an increase in real GDP per capita may offset the price effects. This is evident in scenario one, for instance. Despite the assumption of higher domestic gasoline prices, fuel costs will rise by about 70 percent over the period considered, and gasoline consumption in some of the Gulf states, Saudi Arabia, UAE, and Kuwait will be more than doubled by the terminal year (2010). If domestic prices are assumed to increase by relatively lower rates (scenario two), our equation predicts that gasoline demand will grow by an average annual rate of 5–6 percent in most of these countries.

Fourth, future projections of gasoline demand, while conditional on the assumptions about the exogenous variables, indicate that demand in all the GCC countries (except in Qatar) is expected to rise significantly. Nevertheless, there is a great variation within the Gulf states with regard to future demand levels. This disparity is brought about chiefly by differences in the demand elasticities of income and prices among these countries – the outcome of many factors such as the level of development, size and growth rates of population, magnitude of government energy subsidies, role of multinational oil companies (as refiners and distributors), and geographical area.

Conclusion

In this study we have presented a model to estimate the future demand for gasoline in the GCC countries based on historical data as well as on a set of deterministic variables. Forecasting was performed with the help of six different scenarios regarding economic growth and energy pricing policies. Since energy issues are too complex, and the unknowns too many, it is difficult to forecast energy demand confidently. The growth of the economy, policies designed to affect demand, the resolution of important environmental debates, and changes in energy prices will have dramatic effects on the level of future gasoline demands. Uncertainties associated with these critical elements are great and can never be fully resolved until after the fact. In this exercise, our primary objective has not been to produce a precise forecast based on a single view of the future, rather it has been to indicate the potential dangers of adhering indefinitely to the existing policies which hinder the emergence of the correct market signals.

In addition, a number of messages for policy-making emerged from this analysis. First, further progress in energy efficiency, especially in the transportation sector, would be an important determinant of these countries' future energy balance. Second, as far as gasoline demand is concerned, the study demonstrated clearly that future gasoline demand would be rather high, and that if consumers' attitude toward energy savings were to remain as it is, the growth of consumption could be marked. Third, a sensible energy-pricing policy could help the Gulf countries to manage the adjustment that must be made by providing the incentives to use energy more efficiently. Conversely, holding prices artificially low would aggravate any future energy crisis.

Appendix

Data definition and sources

Our empirical analysis is based on annual data for the period 1970–91. The variables in equation (4) are defined as follows:

G_t = total consumption of gasoline. Gasoline refers to premium and regular varieties.

P_t = the retail price of gasoline is the average cost of premium and regular gasoline and is expressed in local currencies unless otherwise indicated.

GDP represents economic activity in the Gulf Cooperation Council (GCC) countries.

Historical data on gasoline consumption in the GCC were taken from three major sources: the Annual Statistical Abstracts of each country, Organization of Arab Petroleum Exporting Countries, *Annual Statistical Reports*, and International Energy Agency, *Energy Statistics and Balances of non-OECD Countries 1990–91* (Paris: OECD). Data on gasoline prices were obtained by personal communications with the Secretariats of the Organization of the Petroleum Exporting Countries (Vienna) and of OAPEC.

Data on gross domestic product (GDP), exchange rate, population and private consumption were assembled from the Arab Monetary Fund (AMF), *Annual Arab Economic Report* (Abu Dhabi, United Arab Emirates), various issues, and from the International Monetary Fund (IMF), *International Financial Statistics* (Washington, DC), various issues.

CHAPTER 7

Challenges for Gulf Optimization Strategies: Constraints of the Past

Walid Khadduri

After over fifty years of production, the Gulf oil industry continues to play a key role on the world energy scene. This is attributed to the availability of prolific reserves and the low cost of production. However, this position has been challenged in recent years by rising production from outside the Organization of Petroleum Exporting Countries (OPEC), major restructuring and cost cutting by the international oil firms, technological breakthroughs, conservation programs, environmental legislation, and taxation adopted by industrial states.

These events have been accompanied by two major developments: first, the declining influence of OPEC in a new world oil market and second, major changes in the politics and economics of the oil-producing countries that have increased the dependence on oil revenue while at the same time arresting the growth of the national oil industry, rendering it unprepared to meet the ever-changing global developments.

The OPEC members' share of world oil output (including condensates) increased from 28.7 percent to 40.7 percent during the period from 1985 (the year before the oil price collapse) to 1994. Crude oil output of the 12 member states rose from 15.17 million barrels per day (b/d) to 24.85 million b/d during the same period, an increase of 63.8 percent. As for OPEC's exports of crude oil and petroleum products, they rose from 13.1 million b/d to 21.7 million b/d during the years 1985–94, or an increment of 65.6 percent, while its share of world exports rose from 42.9 percent to 52.1 percent over the same span.

As for the future, most projections of oil supply and demand indicate that OPEC members in general, and the Gulf states and Venezuela in particular, will be able to meet most of the incremental demand in the coming years. According to in-house research undertaken by *Middle East Economic Survey* (MEES) editor Ian Seymor, demand for OPEC crude is projected to increase from 25 million b/d in 1995 to 34.5 million b/d in the year 2005, while OPEC crude production capacity is forecast to rise from 28.67 million b/d to 37.65 million b/d during the same period. In other words, OPEC members, and the Gulf states specifically, are well placed to provide the bulk of the additional supplies that the world oil market is projected to demand 10 years from now.

Middle East crudes predominate for the simple reason that the fields in the area continue to be prolific, as shown by the comparison of well productivity for various regions. For example, in 1994, the average productive capacity per well in Middle Eastern OPEC states was 4,082 b/d, compared to 815 b/d in Europe and the Mediterranean, 574 b/d in non-OPEC Middle East, 751 b/d in Africa, 346 b/d in Southeast Asia, 176 b/d in Latin America, and 15 b/d in the United States.[1]

However, despite this comparative advantage and the upbeat projections for the future call on OPEC crude, there is a sense of unease and frustration on the part of the organization's member countries these days. They have seen their oil revenue decline in nominal and real terms and their market share seriously challenged. Moreover, and perhaps more importantly, OPEC states cannot rely on oil revenue to meet their national needs in the same way they were accustomed to in previous decades. While oil revenue was more than enough to meet public budget requirements in the 1970s and 1980s, this is no longer the case. There have been ever-increasing commitments on the part of some and sheer mismanagement of the economy and political rule on the part of others. Domestic pressures have left the OPEC oil industry, and that of the Gulf in particular, at a loss as to which direction it should take: increase production to preserve market share or reduce production below capacity in order to achieve revenue maximization.

External Factors Challenging OPEC

The dilemma that faces OPEC today is a result of the evolution of a number of external factors, mostly not of its own making. These developments have had a direct impact on the oil price that OPEC takes, the production level, and the oil revenue.

OPEC member states have to accept a new range of prices that fluctuate between $13 and $18 per barrel (/b), as compared with the previous, higher range of $16–20/b that prevailed before the Iraqi invasion of Kuwait in August 1990. This new and lower range reflects a price level that allows most international oil firms to remain profitable in the foreseeable future. The anticipated profitability is due, among other reasons, to the reduction in exploration and development costs, accompanied by privatization, deregulation, and the opening up of the upstream sector in a number of countries that had hitherto been closed to international companies. OPEC states have not been able to adjust to the new price levels. The methods customarily used to defend prices, production ceilings, and national quotas, are simply no longer enough to hold prices and stabilize the market.

The former Saudi petroleum minister, Hisham Nazer, summarized the dilemma for OPEC producers when he concluded in a speech in Kuwait in April, 1995, that "there is still a conviction that a mere agreement on ceiling and quotas in OPEC is enough to stabilize a market that is dynamic and diversified by nature." Mr. Nazer explained how the OPEC member states are dealing with the situation:

> It should be noted that while the pace of some changes was fast, the producers were either reluctant or slow to adjust to the new realities, or were applying old tools to a new market framework. For while energy and oil independence were the guiding demand forces, many oil producers continued along the path of oil revenue dependence. Public expenditure continued to increase irrespective of the underlying changes in the oil market and subsequent fluctuations in oil revenues. This dependence ultimately affected in some cases the ability to make decisions in the oil market on their own merits.[2]

The Paris-based International Energy Agency (IEA), in its July 1995 *Oil Market Report*, expects global oil demand to reach 71.2 million b/d in 1996 from 69.6 million b/d in 1995. However, most of the call on the new crude will come from the non-OPEC producers. As a matter of fact, the IEA projected non-OPEC production in 1996 to rise to 43.6 million b/d, a sharp increase of 1.3 million b/d above the 1995 level and some 2.5 million b/d higher than in 1994. The new supplies are to come from faster-than-anticipated growth of production in Colombia, Brazil, and India, higher expected levels of output from California and the Gulf of Mexico, and the decline of production in the former Soviet Union.

These findings were also confirmed by a study published in February 1995, by the London-based financial house Kleinwort Benson. The report concluded that overall, non-OPEC supply is likely to be underpinned by rising output in a number of countries across the globe, as well as by a halt in the drop of production in the United States and Russia, the two largest non-OPEC producers, who together account for around 30 percent of total non-OPEC output.[3] The study projects non-OPEC production in 1995 to increase by at least 800,000 b/d compared to 600,000 b/d in 1994 (Table 7.1). The major increases will be registered in Norway (300,000 b/d), the United Kingdom (100,000 b/d),

Colombia (100,000 b/d), Brazil (90,000 b/d), and Angola (80,000 b/d).

Table 7.I   Major increases in non-OPEC production, 1995 (thousand b/d, including NGLs)

Country	1993	1994	1995
OECD			
Norway	2,370	2,700	3,000
UK	2,190	2,700	2,800
Canada	2,180	2,270	2,330
Australia	557	610	650
Non-OECD			
India	540	635	700
Vietnam	125	140	170
Angola	504	530	610
Oman	790	820	860
Yemen	222	350	380
Syria	560	570	610
Brazil*	880	910	1,000
Colombia	455	460	560
Argentina	595	665	725
Ecuador	341	373	410

*Includes alcohol production of some 200,000 b/d.
Source: Kleinwort Benson, *World Oil Report*, February 1995.

One main reason behind the rise in non-OPEC production is the favorable upstream investment conditions offered, including lower taxes and higher royalty payments that rise in the case of marginal fields to 70 percent of the oil produced in a single year compared to the 30 to 40 percent average of the past. However, what has really made the difference in the past 10 years is the transformation of the business of finding, developing, and lifting oil. Even though oil prices have come down from their highs of over $30/b in the early 1980s, oil firms have been able to achieve large reductions in upstream costs while making substantial profits at the same time.

A study by the New York-based Goldman Sachs of the finding and development costs of 16 major integrated companies revealed that over the 1991–94 period, the collective finding and development costs (excluding purchases and sales) for these firms was reduced from $6.43 per barrel of oil equivalent (boe) to $4.17, or a 35 percent decline over three years.[4] The cost reduction has been achieved because of the extensive use of 3-D seismic analysis, improvements in horizontal drilling techniques, and major advantages in cost-effective development strategies. The critical shift in outlook for the oil industry has been to realize that the profitability of the upstream sector depends largely on maintaining costs in line with prevalent oil prices. This has been made possible by the technological breakthroughs achieved during the past few years.

A clear example of technology's impact has been the development of the offshore areas, where oil production has grown from almost nothing in the early 1960s to a nearly one-third of world oil production at the present time (1995). *And more is on the way, since production can be made from way below the 300 meters of the previous years.*

Today, oil can be lifted from subsea fields at depths of some 1,000 meters of water. Instead of the expensive and environmentally unfriendly concrete blocks and steel structure platforms fixed to the ocean floors, production now is taking place from floating tension leg platform (TLP) designs, as in the case of the Gulf of Mexico, where British Petroleum (BP) and Shell are developing the 42,000 b/d Auger field and the 100,000 b/d Mars field that are to go into production in late 1996.

Most of the recent increase in non-OPEC production has been in the North Sea, particularly Norway. Two examples show why this is the case. The Norwegian firm Norsk Hydro announced last June a major upgrade of the Troll field that more than doubles recoverable reserves and adds in excess of $8 billion to the value of the field. Norsk Hydro attributed this growth to significant advances in oil drilling technology, which led to an expansion in the field's recoverable reserves in excess of 1 billion barrels of oil from 420 million barrels three years ago (when the field was approved for development).[5] The quantum leap in the reserves of one field has meant less geologic risk: the company found additional oil in the same field instead of exploring in virgin territories. Moreover, huge sums of money and time have been saved by using the same production facilities instead of building new ones for different fields.

Norway is taking further measures to find more oil, particularly from marginal and, hence, more expensive fields, as well as to meet the rising cost of fixed platforms and the environmental problems related to them. The Norwegian firm, Statoil, has now ordered a second multi-role crude tanker for delivery in mid-1997. The first such ship, a 103,000-dead weight ton tanker, is set for delivery in November 1996. The multi-purpose ships, which cost around $100 million each, would be used for production, loading, storage, and as conventional crude carriers. They are expected to service a large part of the North Sea crude output in the future as it becomes more difficult to discover large fields. The ships will be positioned near a field and operate there as long as necessary. When the field is depleted, they can either move to another block, without causing serious environmental hazards, or be used as conventional crude carriers. British Petroleum is also using a floating production storage and off-loading vessel (FPSO) to handle output from Schiehallion, the west of Shetlands field with a production capacity of 150,000–170,000 b/d.

OPEC also faces problems on the demand side. Oil consumption has decreased from 54.5 percent of total energy consumed in the countries of the Organization for Economic Cooperation and Development (OECD) in 1973 to 42.2 percent in 1994. Alternative sources of energy are now predominant in the power sector, with gas gradually becoming the major feedstock for new electricity plants. Oil, however, remains predominant in the transport sector. But even here problems lurk ahead.

In early 1994, US President Bill Clinton put a challenge to the heads of General Motors, Ford, and Chrysler to achieve 80 miles-per-gallon fuel consumption in their vehicles. He promised to make available to the American automobile industry the advanced technology now held by the Pentagon in order to achieve this goal. In the meantime, the auto industry already has been working to meet California's strict car emissions standards, which stipulate that by 1998, major auto manufacturers will be required to offer 2 percent of new vehicles sold in that state as zero emission, i.e., electric vehicles (EVs). The share of EVs of the new car sales is legislated to increase to 5 percent by the year 2000 and to 10 percent by 2003. California has already spent over $500 million in its effort to put electric vehicles on the road on time, with more money allocated to meet the designated deadline of 1998. According to the IEA, it is projected that cumulative EVs sales in California by 2003 would be around 370,000 vehicles, and Japan is projected to have 200,000 EVs on the road by the year 2000.[6] While these figures are insignificant compared to the present number of cars in use, the fact of the matter is that EVs are now technically feasible and gradually becoming commercially viable. It is simply a matter of time before local and national authorities make wider use of them, thus constituting a further encroachment on the oil market.

Demand for oil has already been dampened by the taxes imposed on petroleum products in consuming countries. Whereas the price of crude oil has been on a generally declining trend since the 1980s, this has not been felt by the end-user. The imposed taxes have raised the prices of petroleum products in OECD countries (other than the United States and Canada) to over $80/b, whereas OPEC has been left with only a quarter of the per-barrel income. The rise of the environmental movement has accelerated this process in the past few years and given an added excuse to the levying of further taxes. According to a commentary in the May 1995 *OPEC Bulletin*:

> As crude prices fell back in the eighties, taxes were very often applied to mop up the price effect and so dampen demand. Then, as crude prices staged a mild recovery, the environmentalist case provided a convenient camouflage for governments imposing further ad valorem tax rises.[7]

While industry observers have focused their attention since 1973 on OPEC and its ministerial conferences, new forces have emerged that have changed the shape of the markets. The rise of the role and influence of the Wall Street refiners, the reforms in the oil industry itself, the manipulation of commercial and strategic stocks to impact prices, as well as the regional and international politics of the period have all contributed to the changing circumstances and the present marginalization of OPEC's role on the market scene.

What contributed most to the decline of OPEC's influence, however, was perhaps the realization that, while there is oil in the Arab countries, there is no such thing as Arab oil, or Arab oil policy. This phenomenon enabled the industrial states and the International Energy Agency to gradually and systematically reduce the overall influence of OPEC member states over the market and their ability to defend their legitimate national and economic interests.

The end result of these developments has been the expansion of the spot and futures markets for varieties of crude oil, with oil prices behaving like any other commodity. The new market is governed by traders, financial houses, speculators, and global information systems. The role of the OPEC states is largely to defend the floor price. In other words, new players have replaced OPEC in setting day-to-day oil prices. According to Edward Krapels:

> the volume of oil sold in the trading pits at the World Trade Center is three times the size of the volume of physical barrels consumed in the world every day. Add to it the volume of sales in the other paper markets, and the paper oil business is now five to seven times bigger than the physical oil business.[8]

OPEC has relinquished price making to market forces, presumably because the latter is more transparent and offers a better way of assessing prices on a daily basis. The irony of the new market is that it is neither as liquid as it sounds, nor as transparent as its advocates assert. There are over 13 million b/d of crude oil from the North Sea, the Mediterranean, West Africa, and the Middle East, whose prices are assessed daily on the basis of Dated Brent. However, over the past few years, Dated Brent has become increasingly illiquid. Production has steadily declined and the number of Dated Brent cargoes has fallen to an average of one or two a day. Recent legislation by the United Kingdom Oil Taxation Office has also provided less flexibility to integrated producers to sell oil to other parties. The reduced liquidity means:

> that it is now much more difficult for price reporting services to assess where the market is on a given day. It is also much easier for individual companies to

influence the market either inadvertently or deliberately – as a single unrepresentative trade can set the price of Dated Brent if there are no other deals to compare it with. As a result, price assessments have become much more volatile, leading to complaints that the market is being manipulated by some participants.[9]

The same can be said about the two other price markers, Dubai and West Texas Intermediate (WTI).

The Domestic Impediments

Two statements made in September 1994, in Oslo and Lagos, to a large extent demonstrate one of the basic dilemmas currently facing the national oil companies in OPEC members – the gradual loss of comparative advantage as a result of domestic management. On 7 September 1994, Reuters quoted Mr. Thorlief Enger, the Norsk Hydro divisional director for exploration and production, stating in an offshore seminar for investment brokers that his company aims to reduce operation costs at the offshore Oseberg oil field to as low as 80 cents/b in 1995, compared to 87 cents/b in 1994, $1.01/b in 1993, and $1.40/b in 1992.

A day earlier, on 6 September 1994, Reuters reported from Lagos a statement made by the Nigerian Oil Minister Dan Etete to a seminar of petroleum engineers, saying that oil production costs were rising while the price the country was receiving for its crude was falling. According to the Nigerian minister:

> The country is currently facing a serious increase in total production costs in the face of declining crude oil prices . . . the average total production costs ranges between $7–13/b. This is unbelievable and very outrageous, particularly as the incremental barrel from deep water may cost more.[10]

The Nigerian minister did not say why production costs in his country, and for that matter in other OPEC member states, are rising so high when they are declining sharply in other producing countries. The fact is that the oil policies of OPEC member states have remained centralized while there has been major devolution of authority and restructuring in other producing countries and international oil firms. Oil is the main financial revenue and export commodity of the OPEC member states. Major decisions regarding production, prices, investments, senior appointments, and strategic decisions are made by the highest political authority in the states concerned. National oil companies (NOCs) have not been allowed, except in a few cases, to act as commercial enterprises with the authority to make major policy decisions. Moreover, they have had to operate during the past 15 years under difficult conditions. Some have had to endure two regional wars, others sanctions, political upheavals, and economic crises.

The concentration of power and centralization of decision making has been accompanied by related developments that have also impacted adversely on the oil industry in the OPEC member states.

First, there are the widespread phenomena of lack of transparency and absence of accountability. Unlike international oil firms that in most cases are public share-holding firms, obliged by law to report publicly their quarterly and annual accounts, the national oil companies in the OPEC member states keep their budgets and financial operations closed to the public. With the exception of one or two cases, these firms do not announce their plans, budgets, profits, or losses. They only report such matters to other government officials who already are engaged in their plans and policies. Moreover and with few exceptions, the NOCs are not accountable to representative institutions as such bodies frequently do not exist in OPEC states. Furthermore, the limited amount of data that are released by these firms remains sketchy and spotty. Such selective and sporadic release of information cannot provide a comprehensive and true picture of the health of these firms and their actual performance over the years. There is no way an objective comparison can be made, under these circumstances, of the competitiveness of the NOCs with the international oil firms.

The lack of representative governments, proper accountability, and a system of checks and balances has led to waste of resources, lost opportunities, and corruption. This is not surprising. The oil industry is a huge business. Billions of dollars are invested and collected annually. States with absolute and authoritarian rule tend in most cases to mismanage these funds in due course. Senior officials become involved in oil trade and investments for their own personal benefits, depriving the public treasury of its due revenue. This malaise is well known to foreign governments and international firms which, as can be expected, take full advantage of the situation by raising prices in order to meet these costs.

Matters have worsened during the past 15 years. The Iran–Iraq and Gulf wars caused much harm to the local oil industry. The two conflicts have not only destroyed untold numbers of installations and facilities but have hindered the normal growth of the industry and have extracted opportunity costs. The political turmoil in Nigeria and the economic mismanagement in Venezuela have not helped either. As a result, the cost per barrel of OPEC oil increased and the member states' negotiating position weakened. This occurred at a time when other producing countries provided open-door policies and when technology made massive strides in finding more oil at lower costs.

Second, the dramatic developments of the past two decades in many of the OPEC member states have left their imprint on the domestic social and economic scenes. In the case of the Arab oil-producing countries, oil revenue in nominal terms declined from $97.4 billion in 1990 to $81.90 billion in 1994. While the gross domestic product (GDP) in these states rose from $329.7 billion in 1985 to $431.3 billion in 1993, the current account balance declined from a surplus of $78 billion in 1980 to a deficit of $16.7 billion in 1994; the government budgets also registered a sharp decrease from a surplus of $43 billion in 1980 to a deficit of $35.2 billion in 1993 (Table 7.2).

Table 7.2   Selective economic indicators, Arab oil-producing countries, 1980–94 ($bn)

	1980	1985	1990	1991	1992	1993(a)	1994(b)
Net oil export revenue	–	–	97.4	85.4	93.5	87.2	81.9
GDP in current prices	–	329.7	386.6	369.4	407.3	431.3	–
Surplus/deficit in government budgets (c)	43	–36.1	–13.3	–65.6	–41.1	–35.2	–
Balance on current account	78	–1.7	11	–48.6	–15.6	–9.1	–16.7

Notes:
(a) Actual preliminary data
(b) Preliminary estimates
(c) Other than Iraq
Sources: OAPEC, *Annual Report of the Secretary General,* 1994, Kuwait: 1995, pp.53–7. *Unified Arab Economic Report,* 1994, published by the Arab League, AFESD, AMF and OAPEC, Abu Dhabi, 1995.

Moreover, despite the repeated policy statements by OPEC governments to decrease their reliance on oil revenue, the opposite has taken place. In the case of the Arab oil-producing countries, oil revenue's share of total resources increased from 52.6 percent in 1987 to 73.8 percent in 1993, while tax revenue decreased from 28 to 18.6 percent, non-tax revenue fell from 7.2 to 3.6 percent, and investment income dropped from 12.2 to 4 percent, all during the same period (Table 7.3).

Table 7.3   Revenue sources in Arab oil-producing states, 1987–93 (%)

	1987	1988	1989	1990	1991	1992(a)	1993(b)
Oil revenue	52.6	54.0	63.7	76.2	78.7	75.7	73.8
Tax revenue	28.0	28.3	25.4	17.1	17.6	18.2	18.6
Non-tax revenue	7.2	7.1	4.8	5.2	5.0	3.5	3.6
Investment income	12.2	10.6	6.1	1.5	1.3	2.6	4.0

Notes:
(a) Actual preliminary data
(b) Preliminary estimates
Source: *Unified Arab Economic Report*, 1994, p.302.

The data of the past few years also reflect the damaging results of the wars and political tensions that prevailed in the Arab oil-producing countries. The relative share of security and defense expenditure in these states increased from 25.90 percent in 1987 to 28.46 percent in 1993, while public services decreased from 28.64 to 22.58 percent and social services declined from 26.45 to 23.74 percent during the same span (Table 7.4).

Table 7.4   Current expenditures in Arab oil-producing countries, 1987–93 (%)

	1987	1988	1989	1990	1991	1992(a)	1993(b)
Public services	28.64	24.61	28.51	24.44	21.12	21.67	22.58
Security and defense	25.90	28.75	25.42	31.55	24.59	25.42	28.46
Social services	26.45	28.07	23.31	23.46	18.00	21.63	23.74
Economic services	10.50	7.49	9.49	9.89	27.71	21.54	13.33
Others	8.72	10.81	12.49	10.66	8.60	9.74	11.89

Notes:
(a) Actual preliminary data
(b) Preliminary estimates
Source: *Unified Arab Economic Report*, 1994, pp.304–6.

What the statistics do not show is the spillover effect resulting from the deteriorating political conditions in the Middle East and the absence of long-term stability. This is evident in the emigration of thousands of professionals and technocrats, the declining quality of medical and educational services, the lack of investment in public utilities, and thus power cuts and water shortages, the frequent closure of borders among neighboring countries that hinder the growth of regional trade and commerce, and finally, the near absence of any significant foreign investment other than in oil and oil-related activities.

Third, the problems facing OPEC are such that maintaining present policies can only lead to the erosion of both market share and price. The alternatives are not very bright either. OPEC has abandoned price-setting policies, leaving this to the market. Instead, the organization is now in the business of production ceilings and country quotas with the goal of achieving an undetermined optimal price. Even this effort has not been successful. Most OPEC countries (other than Saudi Arabia, the United Arab Emirates, Kuwait, and, of course, Iraq) are producing at capacity, irrespective of their quotas. The dire financial conditions in many of these states are such that the oil authorities cannot resist pressures on them by the finance officials and the heads of states to provide more revenue. The trouble with this logic is that the more member countries pump oil, the less income per barrel they and the rest of OPEC will receive.

In recent years several OPEC member states reversed oil policies and began inviting foreign firms to explore in their upstream sector. They have done so because of cash liquidity problems and the need to substitute for lost capacity as well as to add a new capacity. This situation will result either in restricting the production of the national oil company to the benefit of the foreign partner – a highly likely situation – or in the member country paying lip service to its OPEC quota, which is the most likely outcome. Venezuela is now heading in this direction, along with Nigeria, Qatar, and Algeria. The problem will become more acute and threatening to the cohesion of OPEC when Iraq re-enters the market and invites foreign firms to develop its giant fields on a production-sharing basis with the ultimate aim of producing around 5 million b/d.

There is no question that every member state in OPEC would like to expand production capacity, provided that the right geology and sufficient funding are available to carry out the exploration and development. The problem with this policy is that non-OPEC nations are moving along the same path; they have at their disposal the finance and technology of international oil firms and the support of public and private financial institutions. Moreover, the market continues to see OPEC as the swing producer and considers that, if there are any extra supplies at a particular period, then OPEC alone should shut in capacity, however expensive this may be for its members.

The non-OPEC countries take it for granted that they have no role in defending prices. The conventional attitude is that OPEC was established to defend prices and, therefore, it alone should play the role of the marginal supplier. However, scores of new countries have become oil producers since OPEC was established in 1960. Perhaps the question to be asked is whether it is still practical to expect OPEC to retain its original terms of reference despite the mass of changing circumstances.

It is now routine that the International Energy Agency announces every month what the anticipated call on OPEC crude will be in future months. It does not do the same for non-OPEC crude. The IEA assumes that all the non-OPEC production will come to the market and that there is no need to shut in capacity in this case. This kind of logic finds little support among OPEC officials and technocrats these days and many are questioning the wisdom of such a policy, which keeps OPEC playing the role of swing producer despite its unwillingness to do so.

The problem for OPEC is that it can find very few alternatives to alter the situation. A price war to drive out high-cost producers is not an answer any more. Non-OPEC producers have shown that they can sustain output for a considerable period of time at less than $12/b. It is doubtful, and highly unlikely, that most OPEC states can survive on such a revenue for a long period. Appeals to non-OPEC producers to cooperate and coordinate have fallen on deaf ears. Moreover, discipline within OPEC has become a sad story in itself. So, what are the alternatives and what are the optimal strategies available to the Gulf oil-producing countries in these circumstances?

Looking to Strategies

What this chapter has tried to demonstrate is that, because of exogenous factors in the global petroleum industry, oil revenue in the OPEC member states has reached a plateau. Total oil income has ranged between $93.6 billion in 1987 and $126 billion in 1993 for the 12 member states and is likely to stay in that range for the coming period.[11] The return of Iraq to international trade may even decrease the $100 billion because of the initial nervousness in the market and the negative impact on price. Furthermore, oil rent, the difference between cost of production and the selling price by the producer, is eroding.

As noted earlier, the economic constraints for OPEC started with the price crash of 1986, and were accentuated by the second Gulf war (1990–91). The difficulty, if one can call it that, is one of insufficient oil revenue to meet major capital investments, the rising level of military expenditures, and the ever-increasing social welfare costs – all at the same time. Governments now have to make choices and set priorities. The first reaction has been to freeze major public-sector investments. This measure has already proven that, alone, it is not enough to remedy the situation; more basic economic and political measures are required in order to balance budgets or slow the accumulation of deficits.

How can the Gulf oil-producing states meet this situation? One of the alternatives available to them is to cut the cost of production and enhance their bargaining and negotiating positions, whether through the conclusion of upstream and downstream agreements or through oil sales. Nonetheless, the local oil industry is bearing the burden of domestic factors beyond its control, and there is little the industry can do about it. This includes the lack of regional coordination among the Gulf Cooperation Council (GCC) states themselves, the economic cost of wars, the constraints of the national economies, and corruption. Without a proper handling of these issues, all optimization alternatives become irrelevant to the overall picture.

However, domestic reforms in the GCC economies alone cannot isolate these countries from the difficult conditions of their neighbors. The experience of the Middle East in the past two decades has shown the futility of building fences around oneself and how expensive regional threats and wars can be.

It has been costly, for all concerned, to ignore the national interests of neighboring states. This applies both to how the large regional powers deal with the smaller states and to how the latter should view their future with their bigger and stronger neighbors. All must recognize by now that major global powers assume national security interests in the region and have drawn red lines beyond which local states are not allowed to cross. All must also recognize that armed conflicts have harmed almost all the states and people of the area – did anyone escape the effects of the two Gulf wars that consumed more than a decade? It should be obvious by now that whatever differences may exist – and they are not few – they should be solved by diplomatic means through bilateral negotiations, mediation, arbitration, or international courts.

Finally, the most effective optimization policy available is to widen the economic bases of the oil-producing countries. If oil has lost or is losing its significance as a strategic commodity, and if, for the time being, OPEC cannot play an effective role in setting production and pricing policies, then it follows logically that the organization's member states should not continue to depend overwhelmingly on oil revenue to meet their future expenditures. This means, among other things, opening up their economies to regional trade and the free flow of capital, investment, and services. The GCC states, for example, are already having problems with unemployment, both real and disguised, and the situation is destined to become even worse in the coming decades given the high population growth rate in many of these countries. At least half of the indigenous GCC population is under 15 years of age, with implications for health, education, and job creation. The adoption of a whole new approach to regional relations to increase the opportunities for all the local players can help in meeting this problem. The continuing tension in the region and the lack of a reasonable level of economic relations would aggravate matters even further.

It is doubtful and highly improbable whether such proposals could be instituted in the foreseeable future. The political situation in the region today and the US dual containment policy toward Iraq and Iran do not lend themselves to such alternatives. What is important, however, is to start thinking about them. There is a great need to start introducing fresh ideas to the area and to adopt an innovative approach to domestic and regional issues. Without a new perspective, it is difficult to see how the policies of yesterday can be relevant to and assertive in tomorrow's world, with or without oil revenue.

Conclusion

The preceding chapters have shown that the emerging global economy presents the oil-revenue-dependent Gulf countries with both threats and opportunities regarding their own survival and development. On the demand side, the threats arise from the consequences of measures that were undertaken by the industrialized, oil-importing world in reaction to the two oil shocks of the 1970s. They included successful price-induced energy conservation measures (implemented through fiscal policies and technological innovation) and an increase in the pace of oil discovery and production outside OPEC spurred by the high prices of 1973–74 (through tax incentives and technological breakthroughs). Among other events that have slowed the re-establishment of OPEC and the Gulf as dominant forces in the world energy market are the relatively low economic performance of the industrialized importers (which reduced energy demand in general and oil use in particular) and moves away from oil toward other energy sources, such as natural gas. These factors would not have represented a problem were it not for the risk of oil "obsolescence" for OPEC producers holding huge reserves; less OPEC oil will be needed as more conservation and energy-efficiency measures are put in place, as alternative sources of energy are developed, and as new non-OPEC sources are brought on line to increase world supply.

However, a closer look at the findings of this book reveals that OPEC and the Gulf states may have contributed to their apparent marginalization; past policies of defending prices at all costs (through their role as residual producers) have encouraged other non-OPEC producers to expand their exploration programs, to develop technology to local oil and natural gas in remote areas that were inaccessible a few years ago, and to increase the productivity and longevity of existing oil wells. This has resulted in substantial non-OPEC output capacity. OPEC's residual role in the world oil market has resulted in the present "production-at-will" mentality that prevails in non-OPEC countries and in an OPEC share of world oil output that has only recently begun to recover from the lows of the 1980s. Past OPEC stances seem to have benefited non-OPEC producers more than its own membership. Indeed, there is even evidence that those policies have hurt OPEC more than they helped.

One argument that has recently raised what may be unrealistic hopes among OPEC members regarding future bullish oil markets, especially in those countries with vast reserves (located mainly in the Gulf region), has been that sooner or later supply from non-OPEC sources will taper off and OPEC will resume control of the market. This argument is based on the fact that present non-OPEC reserves are not substantial when compared to those in the Gulf region. The book cautions against the fallacious rationale behind this argument and contends that a careful study of the history of oil since 1945 suggests that this may not be the case.

Several recent developments show that the position of the Gulf in the world oil market is not as prominent as its reserves alone would indicate. Foremost among these is the sizable potential for energy production and exports of the successor states of the former Soviet Union. While there is near unanimity in the literature about the serious state of disrepair and corruption plaguing the FSU's oil industry, thus eliminating any chance for its re-emergence as a major player in the oil market in the short term, a growing number of experts agree that the region is likely to regain its status as a large-scale exporter rivaling the major OPEC producers in about five years. Oil output from the FSU could resume in a substantial way just when supply from other non-OPEC producers (e.g., Britain, Norway, Alaska's North Slope) may start to fall. Obstacles to the resumption of oil exports from the FSU in the near term are largely transient and policy related. In other words, resolution of the difficulties holding back FSU output lies in the medium term. One caveat may be interjected: with a positive economic growth in the FSU, the level of domestic energy demand could resume an upward trend, thereby reducing the FSU's impact on the international oil trade.

While the above-mentioned factors represent external obstacles to the dominance of OPEC and the Gulf region in the world oil market, developments from within the region also threaten to undermine their position. There is mounting evidence that internal oil consumption is growing rapidly and that, unless the trend declines or is reversed, the Gulf will have less crude oil available for export. Just when the Gulf experiences challenges externally due to increased competition from non-OPEC supply, a rising share of its output will be used internally, perhaps resulting in lower foreign-exchange earnings. This scenario would pay off only if there were no new additions to production capacity. One also should keep in mind the diversification drive within the indigenous oil sectors to raise exports of refined products rather than crude only and thereby gain from the added domestic economic activity.

However, the gloomy picture depicted above can be reversed provided the region takes advantage of new developments in the international energy market and the globalization of the world economy. Asia is set for a tremendous spurt of economic growth that will require added sources of energy. The rising Asian energy demand cannot be satisfied with the region's present known energy reserves and output capacity. The potential for energy use in and imports by a booming Asia is considerable. The Gulf region is particularly well positioned to take advantage of this Asian development. However, care should be taken not to assume that the Gulf will automatically reap all or even most of the benefits that an increase in Asian energy demand will generate. Given the Middle East's past experience with hostilities and instability (the Arab–Israeli conflicts, the eight-year Iran–Iraq war, the Iraqi invasion of Kuwait, and the still-to-be-drawn borders), Asia will most likely seek supply security through diversification of the sources of its energy imports and by an aggressive indigenous exploration program. To dampen demand, Asian nations may attempt to limit energy consumption growth through conservation measures and the use of alternative energy sources such as coal, hydro, and solar. The Gulf countries will have to work to alleviate these concerns in order to develop a long-term relationship with the "tigers" and "emerging tigers" of Asia.

Another argument for a potentially brighter future for the Gulf nations emphasizes the fact that the world market has changed in a fundamental way in recent years and that only a thorough understanding of the new emerging framework will lead to successful competition in global oil trade. The new patterns point to the Gulf's greater trading affinity with Asian than with other regions of the world. This contention is consonant with the argument noted earlier about the strategic location of the Gulf in relation to Asian markets.

The new framework also points to a dissonance between the emergence of an international oil market dominated more than ever by economic forces and domestic economies in the oil-exporting countries dominated by political considerations not always in agreement with an optimum allocation of resources. Serious doubts have been raised recently about faulty economic management in OPEC member states that, if not corrected, could lead to disastrous results in the future. High oil prices in the 1970s and 1980s led governments of the oil-revenue-dependent countries to provide lavish welfare benefits for a burgeoning population now accustomed to them. However, as oil prices crashed and stayed low, governments of the oil-exporting nations faced a dilemma: they needed more oil revenues to maintain subsidies (to meet expectations engendered by a generous welfare state) and to sustain a ballooning state bureaucracy while, at the same time, they slashed oil companies' budgets precisely because of dwindling oil revenues and lower foreign-exchange earnings. As non-OPEC production continued to rise and OPEC's share of the world oil market decreased, some countries chose to borrow heavily overseas to sustain their spending habits, hoping that oil prices would resume their upward trend.

This last point raises basic questions about the wisdom behind OPEC's economic policies of the last two decades. It is very clear that management of oil revenues has been disastrous in nations such as Algeria, Nigeria, and Venezuela. For the other OPEC members, great doubt remains about the efficient use of the oil rent windfall. In the case of Algeria, Nigeria, and, to a lesser extent, Venezuela, oil has created more problems than it has solved. The expansion of the oil sector often has seriously weakened viable agriculture and other sectors through the effects of the Dutch disease (appreciation of the real exchange rate in the face of increased foreign exchange earned, brought about by the oil shocks). It also has generated a climate that fostered corruption and allowed blatant mismanagement. To be sure, the other OPEC producers, with the exception of Indonesia, did not have sufficiently diversified economies to experience the effects of the Dutch disease. Moreover, attempts at diversification of an economy frequently limited by the non-hydrocarbon resource base have tended to be in the downstream aspects of the oil industry itself and towards consumption.

In light of the dismal economic performance of OPEC members in the last two decades, some economic thinkers have come to view oil as more of a curse than a blessing, which leads us to question the premises of the preceding chapters – that oil is good not only for the economy, but also for the general welfare of the population, and that the Gulf region should strive to identify what the threats are to its present position and what can be done to thwart those threats. A priori, this premise seems to be based not only on common sense but on a selective review of the development literature, which shows that today's most industrialized countries at various junctures had to rely on leading sectors (railroads in the US, wheat for Canada and Australia, coal for Japan) to trigger their "take-off" stage. However, a closer look at the leading-sector theory shows that, while oil has great potential for triggering or enhancing economic growth, the issue involves moving growth into economic development, which encompasses attributes of sectoral balance, income distribution, and human capital. Can unbalanced growth jump-start balanced development across an economy?

A leading sector is basically one sector of the economy that has a tremendous pull effect economy-wide through direct backward and forward production linkages and through consumption and fiscal linkages. For example, in the United States railroad construction resulted in increased demand for steel (backward linkage) and provided vital transportation links for the rest of the economy (forward linkages). Because oil is a primary commodity largely directed for export in its unprocessed form, direct linkages may be weakened: the backward linkages are non-existent domestically as all machinery required to produce oil is imported. The forward linkages are primarily used as a source of cheap energy and as feedstock for refining and petrochemicals. Although the potential exists for direct linkages, few have been realized given the internal market's size and the lack of economic diversity.

The other two linkages that a leading sector (i.e., oil) could generate are the consumption and fiscal linkages. The former arises when labor that is employed in the production of the leading sector uses its increased purchasing power to generate demand for goods and services from other sectors of the economy. Unfortunately, given the highly capital-intensive nature of the oil industry, which employs only small labor pools, this linkage has been very limited in all oil-exporting countries. If the domestic economy does not itself produce the goods and services demanded, then the income is spent to finance imports.

Oil economies have thus had to rely mostly on the fiscal linkage to generate a development thrust. This linkage operates through the use of oil proceedings as oil revenues to the government. Unlike the other linkages, where market signals guide the spread effects, the fiscal linkage involves a political process that may or may not answer to sound economic advice. As stated earlier, a large portion of oil-generated revenues accruing to the government in oil-based countries was used to create a generous welfare state. Investment was made in development projects and infrastructure, but substantial amounts arising from the exploitation of oil resources were squandered in lavish projects and investment in white elephants. One glaring example of government intervention in the allocation of oil resources is Algeria, where unemployment now hovers around 30 percent and where debt servicing has crippled the economy. Nigeria stands as another case; it is heavily indebted and its per capita income keeps falling year after year. None of the other oil-based countries has fared significantly better than those nations that are deprived of non-hydrocarbon natural resources.

Evidence is mounting that those countries which pursued and relied on sound economic policies rather than on extractive natural resources fared the best; for example, Taiwan, Singapore, South Korea, and Hong Kong, the so-called Asian tigers, all achieved remarkable levels of economic development in a short period of time. What prevented the oil-exporting countries, especially those in the Gulf, from achieving a similar or better growth path? Some have argued that the small population base of the Gulf states represented an obstacle to development because of the domestic market. We know that this argument alone does not survive close scrutiny, as small countries performed well without a large population base (Hong Kong, Singapore, Switzerland, etc.). Yet others warn that the lack of political reforms (the so-called absence of good governance) stands in the way of sustained development in the Third World and in the Gulf region in particular. Here, again, evidence shows that economic development can thrive under differing political regimes: South Korea, Taiwan, and Singapore under authoritarian systems and Hong Kong under the benevolence of British rule. China is making great leaps in development while still under the Communist Party.

This book has not only isolated factors that may adversely affect future Gulf oil exports but has raised fundamental questions about the wisdom of past policies. With the emergence of the global economy, countries dependent upon the exploitation of oil should look to implementing appropriate economic reforms that would position them for the twenty-first century. Attempting to project the oil market 10 or even 20 years forward has most often been a fruitless exercise, given the dismal record of past forecasting. Moving from economies dependent on the export of a single wasting asset (oil) to a self-sustaining economy remains the goal of development. When this becomes a reality, fluctuations in oil prices will lose their ability to inflate or depress national well-being, and oil will be viewed as an input like any other in a broad varied Gulf economy. Under this perspective, the oil price crash of 1986 could be viewed as a wake-up call for OPEC that sudden and dramatic price hikes have negative responses in both supply and demand. The feast-or-famine experience also served to alert the nations heavily dependent on the export of oil that their future was premised upon the consumption of a non-renewable, finite asset; it would be appropriate to think seriously about a post-oil era. Fortunately, larger numbers of decision-makers in the Gulf are aware of the need to diversify the bases of their economic activities, including human resource development, to survive in the emerging and very competitive global economy.

Contributors

Abdul-Razaq Faris Al-Faris is an assistant professor at the Department of Economics at UAE University. He received his Ph.D. from the University of Oxford in 1990. Prior to that, he worked as the head of the Finance Department in the Ministry of Public Works and Housing, and as assistant under-secretary for planning in the Ministry of Education. His publications include: *OPEC and the Market: A Study of Oil Price Rigidity, Determination and Differentials*, and *Military Expenditure in the Arab Countries*, along with several articles on energy and the environment.

Walid Khadduri, executive editor of Middle East Economic Survey (MEES), joined MEES in 1981 after working for seven years as director of information and international relations at the Organization of Arab Petroleum Exporting Countries (OAPEC) in Kuwait. He was also a member of the Political Science Department at Kuwait University (1973–1975) and prior to that had served as director of research at the Institute for Palestine Studies in Beirut (1970–1973). Dr. Khadduri has published extensively in Arabic and English on the oil industry and on the Middle East situation. Dr. Khadduri graduated from the Johns Hopkins University School of Advanced International Studies in 1972 with a Ph.D. in international relations.

Ken Koyama, a senior economist at the Institute of Energy Economics in Tokyo, Japan, is currently a fellow at the Centre for Petroleum and Mineral Law and Policy at the University of Dundee, Scotland. He received his MA in economics from Waseda University in Tokyo, Japan, and has authored numerous articles including "The Gulf Crisis and the Asian Oil Market", "Changes in Japan's Crude Oil Procurement and Its Background", and "Outlook for Oil Supply and Demand in Asia-Pacific Region and Role to be Played by Japan's Oil Industry".

Michael C. Lynch is a research affiliate at the Massachusetts Institute of Technology's Center for International Studies, working in the area of international energy supply and markets, energy policy making, and the role of energy in economic development. With combined SB-SM degrees in political science from MIT, he has been working since the mid-1970s on a variety of studies related to international energy matters, including contributions to the three-volume *International Natural Gas Trade Report* (1985–86). He is widely published in several languages, including the 1989 Economist Intelligence Unit publication *Oil Prices to 2000: The Economics of the Oil Market*, and the 1992 MIT report, *Shoulder Against Shoulder: The Evolution of Oil Industry Strategy*. He is on the council of the United States Association for Energy Economics, and is the program chairperson for their 1996 North American Conference.

Thomas Stauffer is an international oil and finance consultant based in Washington, DC. Educated first as an engineer at MIT and the University of Munich, he later received an MA in Middle East studies and a Ph.D. in economics from Harvard University. He taught economics at Harvard University, the Diplomatische Akademie in Vienna, and the School of Foreign Service of Georgetown University. Dr. Stauffer has been a consultant in the Executive Office of the President, the anti-trust unit of the Federal Trade Commission, the International Energy Agency (Paris), the UNDP, and UNIDO. His specialities include oil and gas taxation, valuation in international law, geopolitics of the Middle East, and comparative energy economics. Dr. Stauffer has produced some one hundred publications dealing with the economics of oil and gas, nuclear power studies, risk and profitability measurement, the geopolitics of the Middle East, and taxation or fiscalization of oil ventures.

Paul Stevens was educated as an economist and as a specialist in the Middle East at Cambridge University and the School of Oriental and African Studies. From 1973 to 1979, he taught at the American University of Beirut interspersed with two years as an oil consultant. In 1979, he began teaching at the University of Surrey where he was a founding member of the Surrey Energy Economics Centre and joint creator of the Third World Energy Policy Studies Group. Since 1993, he has been BP professor of petroleum policy and economics at the Centre for Petroleum and Mineral Law and Policy, University of Dundee, Scotland. Professor Stevens has published widely on energy and development economics and has worked as a consultant for many companies and governments.

Vahan Zanoyan is senior director of the Petroleum Finance Company. In 1987, Mr. Zanoyan founded the Petroleum Finance Market Intelligence Service, which he currently heads. Prior to joining the Petroleum Finance Company, Mr. Zanoyan was a managing director at Wharton, Econometric Forecasting Associates. During his ten years at Wharton, he founded the Middle East Economic Service and served as the company's Resident Specialist on oil markets. Mr. Zanoyan has served as a consultant to numerous major US and foreign oil companies, banks, and other private and public organizations throughout the world. He has over fifteen years of professional experience in analyzing energy markets, production and pricing strategies, and the energy futures market. Educated at the American University in Beirut and the University of Pennsylvania, Mr. Zanoyan has done pioneering work in applied economic analysis of Middle Eastern economies and their development process during the past two decades.

Notes

Chapter 1   The Role of the Gulf in World Energy

1. The discussion here will concentrate on oil exports. There has been very little gas exported from the Arab states of the Gulf. Apart from some minor intra-country trade (Iraq to Kuwait and Southern to Northern Emirates) only the Das Island LNG plant in Abu Dhabi has exported energy outside the region – 4.3 billion cubic meters in 1994 (BP, annual). The reasons for this failure to develop what are undoubtedly large reserves (16.2 percent of world gas reserves in 1994 – BP, annual, *British Petroleum Statistical Review of World Energy* (London: British Petroleum, various editions)) are of great interest, linking into problems with transit pipelines (Paul Stevens, "The Economics of Hydrocarbon Pipelines in the 21st Century," *Pipes and Pipelines International* 29, no. 5 (September–October 1984), pp. 10–14) and problems with LNG (Middle East Economic Consultants, *LNG versus the Methanol Route for Gas Processing in the Arab World* (Beirut: MEEC, 1976)). However, they lie outside the scope of this chapter.

2. As will be explained, some of these "mistakes" were committed by forces external to the region. Often in other cases, given the context, they were virtually pre-ordained and unavoidable.

3. For a more detailed discussion of the framework and its application to explaining oil prices since 1945 see Paul Stevens, "The Determination of Oil Prices 1945–1995: A Diagrammatic Interpretation," *Energy Policy* 23, no. 10 (September 1995); and Stevens, "Oil Prices: The Start of an Era," *Energy Policy* 24, no. 5 (May 1996), pp. 1–12.

4. There is of course no such thing as "the" price of oil. The different quality of crudes means there is a structure of prices reflecting various differentials.

5. Thus, $2.00 in 1950 is equivalent to $12.32 in 1994.

6. This is when crude oil, products or whatever are actually moved between affiliates adjacent to each other in the value chain. This is distinct from financial vertical integration when affiliates are only financially controlled by a parent. Operational vertical integration must also involve financial vertical integration but financial vertical integration may not involve operational vertical integration and may simply rely upon the market to dispose of and secure oil.

7. See M.A. Adelman, *The Economics of Petroleum Supply: Papers by M.A. Adelman 1962–1993* (Cambridge, MA: MIT Press, 1993) and D.G. Sauer, "Measuring Economic Markets for Imported Crude Oil," *Energy Journal*, 15, no. 2 (1994). These issues could be dealt with on a much more elaborate basis; see Stevens, "The Determination of Oil Prices." For example, increasingly, the price in quarterly contracts is set by spot prices of the benchmark crudes. These crudes in turn are subject to local influences – maintenance schedules for Brent, carrying capacity for WTI, etc. See Paul Horsnell and Robert Mabro, *Oil Markets and Prices: The Brent Market and the Formation of World Oil Prices* (Oxford: Oxford University Press, 1993).

8. At various times, key players have been excluded from the market. The Soviet Union was involved only as an exporter of crude and products. Also, the United States increasingly withdrew from the international market and between 1959 and the early 1970s, effectively isolated itself completely.

9. C. Dahl, "A Survey of Oil Product Demand Elasticities," *OPEC Review*, 18, no. 1 (Spring 1994) and D. Hawdon, ed., *Energy Demand: Evidence and Expectations* (London: Surrey University Press, in association with Academic Press, 1992).

10. G. Heal and G. Chichilnisky, *Oil and the International Economy* (Oxford: Clarendon Press, 1991) and K.A. Mork, "Business Cycles and the Oil Market," *Energy Journal* (Special Issue: The Changing World Petroleum Market) (1994).

11. Because base load supply and residual supply are additive, the global supply curve is represented by the residual supply curve.

12. An important difference can be accounted for by the cost of transporting from the wellhead to the export terminal. This can be very significant somewhere like Alaska where the crude must be transported 1,200 kilometers in very difficult conditions. However, in most of these cases, the pipe capacity is contracted on a "take or pay" basis and is therefore part of fixed costs.

13. In reality, for countries with very large reserves, this argument lacked economic validity. At almost any positive discount rate, the present value of oil expected in more than one hundred years is so low that production now rather than later would always be preferable. Delay would be valid only in the presence of a negative discount rate reflecting concern about the societal impact of oil revenues.

14. The oil companies' variable costs will also include their marginal tax payments.

15. This was not entirely due to the embargo but was largely the result of rapidly growing demand in a context where investment in new capacity had slowed (discussed later in this chapter).

16. Paul Stevens, "A Survey of Structural Change in the International Oil Industry 1945–1984," in *The Changing Structure of the World Oil Industry*, edited by D. Hawdon (London: Croom Helm, 1984).

17. It is important to distinguish the range makers from the marginal suppliers in conventional economics terminology.

18. In a perfect world this would be drawn as a vertical line reflecting a fixed supply irrespective of price. In reality, higher prices may encourage the market controllers to relax control and allow production to rise slightly.

19. Others would argue that during the 1970s it was OPEC which fulfilled this role. See G. Gately, "A Ten-Year Retrospective: OPEC and the World Oil Market," *Journal of Economic Literature* 22 (September 1984), pp. 110–14 and J.M. Griffen and D.J. Teece, *OPEC Behaviour and World Oil Prices* (London: George Allen and Unwin, 1982). This author, however, would disagree. See Paul Stevens, "Saudi Arabian Oil Policy: Its Origins, Implementation and Implications," in *State, Society and Economy in Saudi Arabia*, edited by T. Niblock (London: Croom Helm, 1981).

20. Paul Stevens, "OPEC and Oil Revenues," in *Trade, Transfers and Development*, edited by S. Mansoob Murshed and Kunibert Raffer (Cheltenham, UK: Edward Elgar, 1993).

21. In any market, absent a geographically proximate situation, buyers and sellers depend on information about what other buyers and sellers are doing. If there are a small number of players with good information then they, like the Olympian Gods, can see relatively distinct supply and demand curves. They know, at the going price, whether a surplus or shortage exists. They can then behave rationally to achieve their objectives and can decide whether to increase or lower production in order to make the price. In such circumstances, the exact point of intersection is not required to maintain an equilibrium price. Small market imbalances can be ignored and, as illustrated in Figure 1.1, the slopes of the demand curve and production quota line make gaps small over a wide price range. The situation is akin to an insect on water. Surface tension supports a certain weight but above some weight, surface tension breaks and the insect sinks. Thus if the market imbalance was small enough to maintain surface tension, the price held. Only if the gap became too large, would price respond. The job

of the residual supplier was to manipulate the production quota to maintain surface tension. This meant they had to have a price target to which the production quota line could be approximated. This was the price to "make."

22. J. Blair, *The Control of Oil* (London: Macmillan, 1976) and P. Stevens, "A Survey of Structural Change in the International Oil Industry 1945–1984," in *The Changing Structure of the World Oil Industry*, edited by D. Hawdon (London: Croom Helm, 1984).

23. I. Seymour, *OPEC: Instrument of Change* (London: Macmillan, 1980).

24. J. Hartshorn, "From Multinational to National Oil: The Structural Change," *Journal of Energy and Development*, no. 6 (Spring 1980).

25. P. Verleger, "The Evolution of Oil as a Commodity," in *Energy: Markets and Regulation*, edited by R.L. Gordon, H.D. Jacoby, and M.B. Zimmerman (Cambridge, MA: MIT Press, 1987).

26. J. Mohnfeld, "Implications of Structural Change," *Petroleum Economist* (July 1982).

27. J. Roeber, *The Evolution of Oil Markets: Trading Instruments and Their Role in Oil Price Formation* (London: Royal Institute of International Affairs, 1993).

28. It is possible to argue that the production quota line also pivoted to slope down from left to right. At higher prices, cheating seemed less undesirable since it might be believed that the market could take a few more barrels without negative effects on price.

29. J.M. Keynes, *The General Theory of Employment, Interest and Money* (London: Macmillan (Papermac 12), reprinted 1964), p. 156.

30. One of the reasons this history is relevant for the future is that many of these unique characteristics remain true today.

31. A mission led by E.L. DeGoyler, in recognition of the obvious reserve potential of the Gulf reported to the US government in 1944: "the center of gravity of world oil production is shifting from the Gulf–Caribbean area to the Middle East – Persian Gulf area ... and is likely to continue that shift until it is firmly established in that area." Another mission member described the oil reserves as: "the greatest single prize in all history." Quoted in D. Yergin, *The Prize* (New York: Simon and Schuster, 1991), p. 393.

32. M.A. Adelman and M. Shahi, "Oil Development-Operating Cost Estimates, 1955–1985," *Energy Economics* 11, no. 1 (January 1989).

33. G.W. Stocking, *Middle East Oil: A Study in Political and Economic Controversy* (Nashville, TN: Vanderbilt University Press, 1970) and

E.T. Penrose, *The Large International Firm in Developing Countries* (London: George Allen and Unwin, 1968).

34. M.A. Adelman, *The World Petroleum Market* (Baltimore, MD: Johns Hopkins University Press, 1972); H.J. Frank, *Crude Oil Prices in the Middle East* (New York: Praeger, 1966) and Penrose, *The Large International Firm in Developing Countries.*

35. Despite much effort, I have been unable to accurately date this change. It was probably during 1944 – see Blair, *The Control of Oil.*

36. It is interesting to observe that this was because Anglo-Iranian Oil Company (AIOC) refused to reveal to the British government the actual cost of producing products at Abadan. This is interesting not just because Britain was at war at the time but more so because the British government actually owned 51 percent of AIOC.

37. Between 1957 and 1960, the oil companies tried to fight a rearguard action to maintain the link. It was the price cuts of 1959 and 1960 which triggered the creation of OPEC (See Seymour, *OPEC: Instrument of Change*). It is also perhaps significant that following the breaking of the link which potentially opened up the US market to Gulf exports, changes in 1959 to the import regime making imports illegal without a license issued by the secretary of the interior effectively removed the US domestic market from the international oil trade.

38. This was reinforced by the decline in real oil price, which accelerated during the 1960s.

39. The situation was different for refining. The loss of the product output from Abadan did present a serious problem to the industry. Although there were many other factors at work, arguably this was an important driver of the subsequent move to locate refinery capacity away from the fields in the Third World to the industrialized countries. Excess crude producing capacity was cheap and could easily be afforded. The same was not true for refinery capacity. See below.

40. It was also helped by the very large undeveloped finds of oil-in-place which in some cases are still awaiting development.

41. See Paul Stevens, *Joint Venture in Middle East Oil, 1957–1975* (Beirut: Middle East Economic Consultants, 1976).

42. Zaki Yamani, "Participation Versus Nationalization: A Better Means to Survive," in *Continuity and Change in the World Oil Industry*, edited by Z.M. Mikdashi, S. Cleland, and I. Seymour (Beirut: Middle East Research and Publishing Center, 1970).

43. It is necessary to be careful to link higher prices and recession. The first oil shock almost certainly contributed to global recession. The

second oil shock's contribution is more controversial.

44. There is a small amount of excess capacity in Kuwait and Abu Dhabi which is being held back. Venezuela is expanding its capacity quite quickly but appears to be producing it. The controversial subject is Iran. It claims a sustainable capacity of 4 million b/d with a surge capacity of 4.6 million. Many observers, however, suggest it is having serious difficulties in maintaining production at its OPEC quota of 3.6 million b/d.

45. It appears that the offer last March to allow significant amounts of Iraqi oil for humanitarian purposes was made by the US State Department with absolutely no consultation over the implications for the oil market either within the US government or within Saudi Arabia. As a result, Saudi Arabia was rather angry.

46. Paul Stevens, "Arab Downstream Petroleum Exports: Problems and Prospects," in *Middle East Exports: Problems and Prospects*, Occasional Paper Series no. 28 (Durham, UK: Centre for Middle Eastern and Islamic Studies, University of Durham, 1986).

47. Kuwait's refinery developments were aimed more at upgrading capacity.

48. A key argument used to justify the move downstream (both at home and abroad) by some producers is that access to refinery capacity locks in volume to markets and therefore helps reduce volatility.

49. Even so, the realized price of crude oil at the end of the decade was around 20 percent below posted prices. See Seymour, *OPEC: Instrument of Change.*

50. Blair, *The Control of Oil.*

51. Crude long companies also began to look further afield. This was partly to prevent the crude short majors from having a free run at alternative acreage. A more rational approach would have been to encourage the development of the oil-in-place in the Gulf. This, however, appeared to involve a level of "statesmanship" which the companies could not manage (See E.T. Penrose, "Vertical Integration with Joint Control of Raw Material Production: Crude Oil in the Middle East," *Journal of Development Studies*, 1 no. 3 (April 1965)). The argument that diversification of supply sources helps manage future risk of nationalization is doubtful. The same pressures that drove the companies out of the Gulf between 1972 and 1976 were equally at work in other parts of the world.

52. J. Maclean, "The Importance of Newcomers in the International Oil Business, *Middle East Economic Survey*, XI, no. 24 (1968).

53. Stevens, *Joint Ventures in Middle East Oil, 1957–1975.*

54. The most extreme example of this was the decision by Kuwait to invest abroad upstream. Thus, Kuwait investment was going into the creation of cash cows for other governments to milk.

55. Denis Healey, a former British foreign secretary, once coined his first law of holes: "when you are in one, stop digging." The Gulf producers breached that law.

56. Stevens, *Joint Ventures in Middle East Oil, 1957–1975.*

57. Seymour, *OPEC: Instrument of Change.*

58. The significance of this was that it was the first time the producers had unilaterally set price. Up to September 1970, it had been the prerogative of companies, and between September 1970 and October 1973, the outcome of negotiations between companies and producer governments.

59. Stevens, "Oil Prices: The Start of an Era."

60. This does not always work. For example, in the UK when the chancellor of the exchequer tried to introduce sales taxes on residential gas and electricity sales it was rebuffed. His claim that the measures were driven by environmental concern rather than revenue requirements was greeted with virtually universal derision.

61. International Energy Agency (IEA), *World Energy Outlook* (Paris: IEA, OECD, 1995); World Energy Council, *Energy for Tomorrow's World: The Realities, the Real Options, and the Agenda for Achievement* (New York: St. Martin's Press, 1993).

Chapter 2   A Relevant Framework for Understanding the Global Crude Oil Market

1. The reference is to OPEC's past role in shaping short-term prices, not to its *ability* to influence oil prices in any particular predetermined direction. While OPEC's attempts to fine-tune supplies affected oil prices, there was no demonstrated ability on the part of the organization to achieve any production or price targets.

2. The more sophisticated refineries – i.e., those with higher desulfurization and upgrading capacity – can handle heavier and more sour crude grades and produce more valuable lighter end products. Thus, refinery complexity is an important determinant (from the demand side) of the pattern of flows of different grades of crude oil.

3. Also, any attempt to change the overall ceiling would have run into
 • serious quota bickering within OPEC, and it was good to keep that issue

on ice for a while. With almost every OPEC and non-OPEC country already producing at or close to full capacity, and with the prospects for significant additions to production capacity in either group assumed to be small, the "hope" was that, with rising demand, demand for OPEC crude would also rise.

4. For a more detailed analysis of the seasonality syndrome, see *One Price for All Seasons: The Diminishing Seasonality of Oil Markets*, a special report published jointly by the Petroleum Finance Company and *Petroleum Intelligence Weekly*, September 1993.

5. The production capacity lost between 1991 and 1995 from the FSU and Iraq alone amounts to over 8 million b/d.

Chapter 3   Energy Demand in Asian Countries

1. The 11 Asian countries are Japan, Republic of Korea (ROK), Taiwan, China, Hong Kong, Singapore, Indonesia, Malaysia, Thailand, the Philippines, and India.

2. To obtain this result, the reserves of Australia and New Zealand were deducted from the total reserves of Asia and Australasia shown in the *BP Statistical Review of World Energy*.

3. For example, proved reserves are defined as "those quantities which geological and engineering information indicate with reasonable certainty can be recovered in the future from known reservoirs under existing economic and operational conditions" in the *BP Statistical Review of World Energy*.

4. Other than fossil fuels, many Asian developing countries are considered to have substantial potential for hydro-power generation, taking account of the numbers of rivers without dams for hydro-power generation and abundant rainfalls in the tropical areas in Asia. As for uranium resources, India, China, ROK, Japan, and Indonesia combined have 4.6 billion tonnes of uranium resources according to the "Survey of Energy Resources 1992" by the World Energy Conference.

5. The geographical definition for Asia in this part follows the International Energy Agency's definition. Asia in this part comprises Japan and all non-OECD Asian countries.

6. It is important to note, however, that many of these new grass-roots LNG projects face difficult situations from an economic standpoint, as previously mentioned.

7. For example, oil exports from the US (Alaska), for which the removal of existing export bans is now being considered by the US

government, can be a source of diversification of oil imports to Asian countries. In addition, increased oil imports from oil producers in Latin America like Colombia and Venezuela, in West Africa like Angola and Gabon, in the North Sea, and so on can be a source of diversification. As for natural gas, see Table 3.11.

8. The energy market, including the gas market, is currently undergoing deregulation in many Asian countries. However, the downstream gas market is one of the markets where strong regulations remain and complete deregulation on new entry is quite unlikely.

9. In reality, the inter-fuel competition in the power generation sector is often restricted in many Asian countries, as governments often give priority to certain types of power generation, such as nuclear and coal-fired.

10. These policies and strategies have not been specifically to restrict Gulf penetration. However, there is good reason to suppose that the implicit target of policies and strategies might have been to restrict "Gulf" penetration, as the past energy (oil) crises have their origins in the Middle East, including the Gulf.

11. Please note that these projects for grass-roots refinery construction are facing difficult conditions from an economic standpoint, as are new grass-roots LNG projects.

12. China implemented a series of liberalization policies for oil imports, pricing, and distribution in the early 1990s to cope with its rapidly increasing oil demand and import requirements. But as liberalization has progressed, a number of problems have emerged such as the selling of oil products through illegal channels and the wide fluctuation of oil products prices, often above international price levels. To restore order in the overheated and confused markets, China banned oil product imports in 1994 in order to strengthen central government controls on the domestic oil industry. They implemented a series of belt-tightening policy measures in May 1994, such as restrictions on oil product pricing and distribution.

Chapter 4   Natural Gas and Gulf Oil

1. Processing costs for recovering NGLs vary widely, depending upon the richness of the gas stream and the percentage of the cut. Twenty to thirty-five percent of gross receipts is a representative range, but the actual costs – and hence the net value of NGLs – is situation-specific. Those costs are subsumed in the costs of an LNG plant where wet gas is the feed.

2. The balance in North America is less clear; there replacement economics are driven primarily by E&D costs, not transportation costs.

3. Japan subsidized LNG imports by a comparable amount per Mcf, but the affected volumes are substantially less.

4. The small volumes of LNG imported by the US are used primarily for peak-shaving, winter service.

5. Relative efficiencies of use are ignored. LNG into combined-cycle power plants would displace rather more oil from a competing oil-fired steam plant.

6. Illustrative calculations can be found in International Energy Agency, *Oil Gas & Coal: Supply Outlook* (Paris: International Energy Agency, 1985).

7. The issue of gas pricing figures in current disputes over possible subsidization of energy-intensive exports from oil-producing countries. The argument that gas should be priced at or near crude oil equivalency is fallacious where the opportunity costs are low or zero.

8. Exporting countries differ in this regard; the opportunity cost of gas in Egypt, for example, is close to that of exportable fuel oil, since near-term supply is less than potential demand. Similarly, the value in Bahrain, where supplies are limited, is also relatively high.

9. T.R. Stauffer, "Energy-Intensive Industrialization in the Middle East: Third World Opportunities," (*UNIDO/IS* 482, Vienna, 28 August 1984), pp. 1-50 (also published in *Industry and Development*, no.14, New York, 1985).

10. The fuel cost advantage, however, is partly offset by the higher costs of shipping clean products, or heavy fuel oil, compared with crude oil.

11. There is a small tradeoff against oil. Some oil has been injected to supplement coke in blast furnaces. That use depends upon capacity constraints in the mills (oil injection increases throughput) and the relative prices of heavy fuel oil and metallurgical coke.

12. Revenues attributable to returns to capital, whether domestic or foreign, must be deducted in calculating the netback values, or resource revenues, at the wellhead. The value of the derivative liquids is discussed elsewhere.

13. Subsidies also promoted LNG imports into Japan.

Chapter 5   The Economics of Petroleum in the Former Soviet Union

1. Executive Director, Working Group on Asian Energy and Security, Center for International Studies, Massachusetts Institute of Technology.

2. Saudi Arabia is the largest producer (at 9 mb/d in 1994) and the United

States is second largest producer at 8.4 mb/d in 1994, leaving the FSU third at 7.4 mb/d in 1994. Saudi Arabia is also the largest exporter, at 7.5 mb/d, followed by Iran (2.5), and Venezuela, Nigeria, and Norway, each at about 2 mb/d in 1994. See BP, *BP Statistical Review of World Energy* (1995) and *International Energy Annual: 1993* (1995).

3. Production dropped by 5 mb/d from 1988 to 1994, and consumption fell by 4.3 mb/d in the same period. See BP, op. cit.

4. Note that most forecasts combine E. European production with that from the former Soviet Union, but with FSU production approximately 25 times that of E. Europe, there is little impact from uncertainty about possible E. European production levels.

5. Note that for the International Energy Workshop survey, the mean is shown for all forecasts, and excluding the GRREF, which is an outlier, possibly due to definition problems (i.e., including other former socialist countries with the FSU).

6. Many of the arguments supporting forecasts of continually rising prices seemed quite logical and appeared to stand on their own, although they have proved to be very much in error. See Michael Lynch, "The Fog of Commerce, Long-Term Oil Market Forecasting," (working paper, Center for International Studies, September 1992).

7. Ibid.

8. This has been seen repeatedly in oil supply forecasting, where the method of aggregating reports of large field developments nearly always resulted in production forecasts which were too low. See Michael Lynch, "The Analysis and Forecasting of Petroleum Supply: Sources of Errors and Bias," (Paper delivered to the Eighth International Symposium on Energy Modeling, Institute of Gas Technology, Atlanta, GA, April 1995).

9. CIA, *Prospects for Soviet Oil Production,* April 1977.

10. CIA, *The International Energy Situation, Outlook to 1985,* April 1997, and *The World Oil Market in the Years Ahead,* August 1979. Some argued that this situation would necessitate a Soviet invasion of Iran, and the US Rapid Deployment Force was created in response.

11. Oil-in-place refers to all oil in the ground, only a fraction of which will actually be produced, depending on geology and production methods. In Russia, typically one-fifth to one-third has been produced historically, meaning that a report of field size using oil-in-place may be exaggerated by three to five times, although in the long run, recovery tends to increase. Consider Prudhoe Bay, which has about 30 billion barrels of oil-in-place, but slightly over 10 billion barrels of recoverable oil. See

Nehring, *Giant Oil Fields and World Oil Resources,* RAND Corporation R-2284-CIA, June 1978.

12. The term resource is used here to equate with the more scientific term, "ultimately recoverable resources," or URR, which refers to the total amount of petroleum which can be recovered at the current price and technology, i.e., past production, current proved reserves, and undiscovered oil. Changing estimates reflect changing geological knowledge, technological improvements, and possibly psychology.

13. Note that the extremely high proportion of the Middle East's oil which is estimated to be already discovered by the USGS illustrates two shortcomings these estimates possess. First, the proved reserves in some Middle East countries are believed exaggerated to reflect OPEC's effort in the late 1980s to set quotas based on supposedly objective factors like reserves and production capacity. However, even this would only account for a small fraction of the difference between the US and the Middle East given that there have been only 1.4 percent as many wells drilled per 100 sq. km of sedimentary basis in the Middle East as in the US, implying that there is a methodological error, or bias towards conservatism. In fact, the current estimate of Middle East resources is already far beyond what was thought to be extremely unlikely by Masters et al., 1983 (see Bibliography).

14. A perusal of the trade press finds much support for this thesis. For example, Amoco is cited as saying that many fields of 200–300 million barrels are to be found in the offshore arctic regions, viable at a $15/bbl price. Already, three finds over 200 mb have been made in the Pechora Sea (*Petroleum Intelligence Weekly,* 16 May 1994). Individual fields are described in Table 5.6.

15. Note that Dienes et al. include 1991 data, but the drop is so sharp in well productivity compared to prior years that transient factors, possibly including misreporting, are more likely to be responsible than geological conditions. See Leslie Dienes, Istvan Dobozi, and Marian Radetzki, *Energy and Economic Reform in the Former Soviet Union* (New York: St. Martin's Press, 1994).

16. *Oil and Gas Journal,* 30 August 1993, p. 31.

17. See Chuck E. Shultz, "Oil in the CIS," (Twelfth CERI International Oil and Gas Markets Conference, Calgary, Alberta, 27 September 1993), p. 6. Note that average Third World, non-OPEC well productivity is about 300 b/d/well.

18. See the *Izvestia* story cited in *Oil and Gas Journal,* 3 July 1989, p. 18, or *Petroleum Intelligence Weekly,* 19 February 1990, p. 2.

19. Dienes, et al. (1994), p. 52, estimated that 350 million barrels are unrecoverable from 33 large reservoirs in W. Siberia, suggesting that the total national losses are extraordinary.

20. Dienes, et al., p. 73, calculates transport costs as less than $1/ton historically, and unlikely to go above $2/ton by 2000. The IEA, 1994, p. 41, shows transport costs as never more than $4–5/ton. See International Energy Agency, *Russian Energy Prices, Taxes and Costs* (Paris, 1994).

21. Knowing the breadth, depth, or impact of data falsification is impossible, but there have been numerous anecdotal reports on the subject. Some CIA analysts were reported in 1988 to believe that the government understated earlier economic growth to make Gorbachev look better. (*New York Times,* 2 November 1988, A9). Also, *The Wall Street Journal,* 15 August 1989, A10, cited reports of organizations understating sales to hide the affluence. Kornai describes in theoretical terms how socialism leads rational actors to hoard materials and labor, which distorts both demand and cost figures. See Janos Kornai, *Contradictions and Dilemmas: Studies on the Socialist Economy and Society* (Cambridge, MA: MIT Press, 1986).

22. Michael Lynch, "Oil Capacity Costs and Prices in the 1990s," (Washington International Energy Group Monograph, July 1990).

23. Capacity costs are commonly used in the industry, since capital costs and capacity added are the data which are most available. They are primarily of comparative value, since translating them into wellhead costs (comparable to selling prices), requires knowledge of discount rates and depletion. These two factors can be assumed, but accuracy is reduced. Marginal costs represent the cost of additional or incremental production, and are wellhead costs. Thus, they can be compared to selling prices to determine the profitability of new investment under the existing fiscal regime. Average costs, which are less important, indicate the cost of existing production, and show the approximate profitability of the industry, where taxes and prices are known. In most of the cases cited in Table 5.8, the methodology of the authors is not known and it is possible that there are discrepancies in the definition of type of costs.

24. Summarized in M. A. Adelman and Michael C. Lynch, "Natural Gas Supply in Western Europe," in *Western Europe Natural Gas Trade* (Final Report of the International Natural Gas Trade Project, MIT Energy Laboratory, December 1986, Appendix B).

25. *Petroleum Intelligence Weekly,* 29 May 1995, p. 4 and *Oil and Gas Journal,* 26 June 1995, p. 22.

26. While this may sound primitive, there are also buildings at MIT where this is practiced.

27. Dienes, Dobozi, and Radetzki, chapter 3, especially pp.134–6. They have corrected for the fact that the FSU economy includes large amounts of energy-intensive heavy industry, an area in which the post-Soviet economy should continue to have a comparative advantage, suggesting that per-capita or per-GNP energy usage may continue to be greater than in other countries at a comparable stage of development, all else being equal.

28. Ukraine has demanded transit fees far beyond what are normally paid in other countries, equal to about 8 cents/MMBtu per 100 kilometers, stating that this will not even provide recovery of operating and capital costs, WGI, 30 June 1995, p. 4. In fact, it is substantially above typical costs in other countries, while the depressed economy in the Ukraine would suggest they should be significantly below them. Presumably, these demands reflect only an attempt to utilize the bargaining power inherent in the in-place investment of the existing pipeline, although this doesn't mean they won't receive their demands.

29. Note that Dienes et al., p. 77, refer to studies showing substantial increases in costs, especially if production increases, and Grace argues that smaller fields will raise cost substantially over time. See John D. Grace, "Cost Russia's biggest challenge in maintaining gas supplies," *Oil and Gas Journal,* 13 February 1995. While increased depletion of a fixed resource may drive up costs, all else being equal, it is not clear why a 33 percent increase in production would mean a quadrupling of transport costs and a greater relative increase in extraction costs. (Note that other gas producers, such as the US and Canada, have experienced larger production increases without these levels of cost inflation. See Adelman and Lynch, 1985.) The nature of the analysis is not clear, but the results probably reflect extrapolating of the rising costs experienced during the 1980s crash programs, with all of their inefficiencies, and ignoring the benefits of improving factor productivity (vs geological) and infrastructure. See Lynch, "The Analysis and Forecasting of Petroleum Supply ...".

30. China consumed 600 bcf of natural gas in 1994, according to BP, 1995. If gas held the same market share in China as it does in Japan, consumption would more than quintuple, necessitating the equivalent of current FSU exports to Western Europe.

31. *Petroleum Intelligence Weekly,* 10 July 1995, p. 5.

32. *Petroleum Intelligence Weekly*, 3 February 1995, p. 3 gives the 1.2 mb/d figure; CGES, May–June 1995, the 2.25 mb/d.
33. "A Crude business in Russia," *The Economist*, 25 May 1996, p. 68.
34. See *Petroleum Intelligence Weekly*, 6 May 1996, p.3.
35. *The Economist*, 18 April 1992, p. 75.
36. Predicting and planning for changes in differentials has repeatedly been a problem for the oil industry. In both the late 1970s and late 1980s, companies anticipated widening differentials and built so much refinery upgrading that differentials collapsed, making the upgrading unprofitable. See Michael Lynch, "Shoulder Against Shoulder, The Evolution of Oil Industry Strategy," Centre for International Studies Working Paper, December 1994 for a description of this.
37. Richard J. Samuels, *The Business of the Japanese State: Energy Markets in Comparative and Historical Perspective*, (Ithaca, NY: Cornell University Press, 1987).

Chapter 6   Forecasting the Demand for Gasoline in the GCC Countries

1. See A. Al-Faris, *The Demand for Gasoline in the GCC Countries* (Kuwait: Industrial Bank of Kuwait) IBK Papers, no. 39 (December 1993).
2. For a discussion of these methods, see B.L. Bowerman and R.T. O'Connell, *Time Series Forecasting: Unified Concepts and Computer Implementation* 2nd ed. (Boston: Duxbury Press, 1987).
3. S.S. George, "Energy Forecasting Techniques: An Overview," in T.H. Morlan (ed.), *Energy Forecasting, Proceedings of a session sponsored by the energy division of the American Society of Civil Engineers in conjunction with the ASCE Convention in Detroit, Michigan* (24 October 1985), p. 18.
4. A detailed description of the model can be found in Al-Faris, *The Demand for Gasoline*, and A. Al-Faris: "Income and Price Elasticities of Gasoline Demand in the OAPEC Countries," *Journal of Energy and Development*, 17, no. 2 (1993).
5. See M.C. Lynch, *The Fog of Commerce: The Failure of Long-term Oil Market Forecasting* (MIT: Center for International Studies Working Paper, September 1992).

Chapter 7   Challenges for Gulf Optimization Strategies

1. CS First Boston, *Global Energy Resources* (New York, 28 April 1995), p. 4.
2. Hisham Nazer, "Challenges for the Oil Producers into the 21st Century," lecture delivered at the Second International Conference on

Catalysts in Petroleum Refining and Petrochemical Industries, Kuwait, 22 April 1995, reprinted in *Middle East Economic Survey*, 1 May 1995.

3. Kleinwort Benson, *World Oil Report* (London: Kleinwort Benson, February 1995).

4. Goldman Sachs, *Finding Costs and Reserve Replacement Results, 1980–1994* (New York; Goldman Sachs, 25 May 1995), pp. 1–5.

5. *Financial Times*, 29 June 1995.

6. International Energy Agency (IEA), *World Energy Outlook* (Paris: IEA, 1995), p. 287.

7. *OPEC Bulletin*, May 1995.

8. Edward N. Krapels, "From OPEC to Futures Markets: A New Government Structure for International Oil," *Petroleum Politics*, 5, no. 2, 1994, pp. 3–4.

9. *Weekly Petroleum Argus*, 21 August 1995.

10. *Reuters*, 6 September 1995.

11. OPEC, *Annual Statistical Bulletin 1993*, OPEC, Vienna, 1994, p. 6.

Bibliography

Adelman, Morris A. *The World Petroleum Market*. Baltimore, MD: Johns Hopkins University Press, 1972.

— *The Economics of Petroleum Supply: Papers by M.A. Adelman 1962–1993*. Cambridge, MA: MIT Press, 1993.

— and Michael C. Lynch. "Supply Aspects of North American Gas Trade." In *Canadian–U.S. Natural Gas Trade*, Final Report of the International Natural Gas Trade Project, MIT Energy Laboratory Report 85-013, October 1985.

— "Natural Gas Supply in Western Europe." In *Western Europe Natural Gas Trade*, Final Report of the International Natural Gas Trade Project, MIT Energy Laboratory, December 1986.

— and Shahi Manoj. "Oil Development-Operating Cost Estimates, 1955–85." *Energy Economics* (January 1989).

Al-Faris, A.F. "Income and Price Elasticities of Gasoline Demand in the OAPEC Countries." *Journal of Energy and Development* 17, no. 2 (1993).

— *The Demand for Gasoline in the GCC Countries*. Kuwait: Industrial Bank of Kuwait, IBK Papers, Series no. 39 (December 1993).

American Petroleum Institute (API). "Petroleum Import and National Security: Discussion Paper #405." Washington, DC, 1985.

— "Energy Security White Paper: U.S. Decisions and Global Trends." Washington, DC, 1988.

Baltagi, B.H., and J.M. Griffin. "US Gasoline Demand: What Next?" *Energy Journal* 5, no. 1 (1984).

Baumgartner, T., and A. Midttum, eds. *The Politics of Energy Forecasting: A Comparative Study of Energy Forecasting in Western Europe and North America*. Oxford: Clarendon Press, 1987.

Blair, John. *The Control of Oil*. London: Macmillan, 1976.

BP. *British Petroleum Statistical Review of World Energy*. London: British Petroleum, annual.

— *BP Statistical Review of World Energy 1995*. London, 1995.

CIA. *Prospects for Soviet Oil Production*, April 1977a.

— *The International Energy Situation: Outlook to 1985*, April 1977b.

— *The World Oil Market in the Years Ahead*, August 1979.

Crook, Leo. *Oil Terms*. Wilton House Publications, 1975.

CS First Boston. *Global Energy Resources*. New York, 28 April 1995.

Dahl, Carole. "A Survey of Oil Product Demand Elasticities." *OPEC Review* XVIII, no. 1 (Spring 1994).

Darmstadter, Joel, with Perry D. Teitelbaum and Jaroslav G. Polach. *Energy in the World Economy*. Baltimore, MD: Johns Hopkins University Press, 1971.

Deagle, E.A. and B. Mossavar-Rahmani. *Oil Demand and Energy Markets: An Interpretation of Forecast for the 1980s*. Harvard Energy Security Program, J.F. Kennedy School of Government, Harvard University, Discussion Paper Series, H-82-03 (May 1982).

Department of Commerce (DOC). "The Effect of Crude Oil and Refined Petroleum Product Imports on the National Security." Washington, DC, 1998, 1994.

Department of Energy (DOE). "Energy Security: A Report to the President of the United States." Washington, DC, 1987.

Dienes, Leslie, Istvan Dobozi, and Marian Radetzki. *Energy and Economic Reform in the Former Soviet Union*. New York: St. Martin's Press, 1994.

Frank, Helmut J. *Crude Oil Prices in the Middle East*. New York: Praeger, 1966.

Fried, Edward R., and Philip H. Trezise. "Oil Security: Retrospect and Prospect." Brookings Institution, Washington, DC, 1993.

Fujii, Hideaki. "Kankoku no Sekiyuseihin no Kakakukisei ni Tuite" (Regulations on Oil Product Pricing in South Korea). *Kokusai Enerugi Doukou Bunseki* (International Energy Analysis). Tokyo, Japan: Institute of Energy Economics (July 1995).

Fujime, Kazuya. "21 Seike no Enerugi Josei" (Energy Situations in the 21st Century). *Enerugi Keizai* (Energy Economics). Tokyo, Japan: Institute of Energy Economics (1995).

Gately, Demot. "A Ten-Year Retrospective: OPEC and the World Oil Market." *Journal of Economic Literature* XXII (September 1984).

George, S.S. "Energy Forecasting Techniques: An Overview." In *Energy Forecasting,* edited by T.H. Morlan. New York: American Society of Civil Engineers, 1985.

Goldman Sachs. *Finding Costs and Reserve Replacement Results, 1980–1994*. New York: Goldman Sachs, 25 May 1995.

Grace, John D. "Cost Russia's biggest challenge in maintaining gas supplies," Oil & Gas Journal (13 February 1995)

— and Wayne Beninger. "Idle Wells: A Cost/Benefit Analysis." *Russian Petroleum Investor* (July 1993).

Griffen, James M., and David J. Teece. *OPEC Behaviour and World Oil Prices*. London: George Allen and Unwin, 1982.

Gustafson, Thane. *Crisis Amid Plenty: The Politics of Soviet Energy under Brezhnev and Gorbachev*. Princeton, NJ: Princeton University Press, 1990.

Hartshorn, Jack. "From Multinational to National Oil: The Structural Change." *Journal of Energy and Development* 6 (Spring 1980).

Hawdon, David, ed. *Energy Demand: Evidence and Expectations*. London: Surrey University Press in association with Academic Press, 1992.

Heal, Geoffrey and Graciela Chichilnisky. *Oil and the International Economy*. Oxford: Clarendon Press, 1991.

Hogan, William W. "Energy Security Revisited." Cambridge, MA: Harvard University Energy and Environmental Policy Center, 1987.

Horsnell, Paul and R. Mabro. *Oil Markets and Prices: The Brent Market and the Formation of World Oil Prices*. Oxford: Oxford University Press, 1993.

Ibrahim, I. "Energy Forecasting and Energy Data in the Arab Countries." *OPEC Review* (Summer 1985).

Institute of Energy Economics, Japan (IEE). "Chugoku Oyobi Minami Asia (India, Pakistan, and Bangladesh) so Sekiyu Jijou" (Oil Situations in China and South Asian Countries: India, Pakistan, and Bangladesh). *Kenkyu Chosa Houkokusho* (Study and Research Report), no. 260, Tokyo, Japan: Institute of Energy Economics (1994).

International Energy Agency (IEA). *Energy Statistics and Balances of non-OECD Countries* 1990–91. Paris, 1993.

— *World Energy Outlook*. Paris, 1993.

— "Energy Statistics and Balances of non-OECD Countries." Paris, 1994.

— "Energy Statistics of OECD Countries." Paris, 1994.

— *Russian Energy Prices, Taxes and Costs*, Paris 1994.

— *Oil, Gas & Coal Supply Outlook*, Paris, 1995.

— *World Energy Outlook*. Paris: International Energy Agency, OECD, 1995.

Itabashi, Kenji, and Yuji Ichino. "Current Status of Energy and Environment-Related Problems in Asia and Roles to be Played by Japan through International Cooperation Centering on Air Pollution." *Energy in Japan*. Tokyo, Japan: Institute of Energy Economics (1994).

Kanayama, Hisahiro. "Energy Problems in China." *Asia-Pacific Review* 2, no. 1, Institute for International Policy Studies, Tokyo (1995).

Keynes, John M. *The General Theory of Employment, Interest and Money*. London: Macmillan (Papermac 12), repr. 1964.

Kleinwort Benson. *World Oil Report*. London: Kleinwort Benson, February 1995.

Koide, Yasuhiro. "Saikin no Asia Shokoku no Sekiyu Jijou (1): China,

Republic of Korea and Taiwan" (Recent Oil Situations in Asian Countries (1): China, Republic of Korea and Taiwan). *Kokusai Enerugi Doukou Bunseki* (International Energy Analysis). Tokyo, Japan, Institute of Energy Economics (1994).

— "Kisei Kanwa to Wagakuni Sekiyu Sangyou no Shourai" (Deregulation and Future of Japan's Oil Industry). *Enerugi Keizai* (Energy Economics). Tokyo, Japan: Institute of Energy Economics (1995).

Kornai, Janos. *Contradictions and Dilemmas: Studies on the Socialist Economy and Society.* Cambridge, MA: MIT Press, 1986.

Koyama, Ken. "Saikin no Asia Shuyoukoku no Sekiyu/Enerugi Juyou Doukou to Kongo no Tenboou" (Recent Trends and Outlook for Oil and Energy Demand in Asian Countries). *Kokusai Enerugi Doukou Bunseki* (International Energy Analysis). Tokyo, Japan: Institute of Energy Economics (1992).

— "International Oil Supply/Demand Perspectives and Japan's Subjects in Crude Oil Procurement." *Energy in Japan.* Tokyo: Institute of Energy Economics, Japan (1993).

— "Outlook for Oil Supply and Demand in Asia-Pacific Region and Role to be Played by Japan's Oil Industry." *Energy in Japan.* Tokyo: Institute of Energy Economics, Japan (1995).

Krapels, Edward N., "From OPEC to Futures Markets: A New Government structure for International Oil." *Petroleum Politics* 5, no. 2 (1994).

Lichtblau, John H. "Oil Import and National Security: Is there still a Connection?" New York: Petroleum Industry Research Foundation, 1994.

Lynch, Michael C. "Oil Capacity Costs and Prices in the 1990s." Washington International Energy Group Monograph (July 1990).

—"The Fog of Commerce: The Failure of Long-Term Oil Market Forecasting." Working Paper, Center for International Studies, September 1992.

—"Shoulder Against Shoulder: The Evolution of Oil Industry Strategy." Center for International Studies, Working Paper, December 1994.

— "Penetrating the Enigma: Predicting Energy Supply and Demand in the Former Soviet Union." SNS Energy Occasional Paper no. 70, Stockholm, January 1995a.

—"Cost of Delivering East Siberian Gas to Japan." Paper delivered to the International Conference on Northeast Asian Natural Gas Pipeline, Tokyo, March 1995b.

—"The Analysis and Forecasting of Petroleum Supply: Sources of Errors and Bias." Paper delivered to the Eighth International Symposium on Energy

Modeling, Institute of Gas Technology, Atlanta, GA, April 1995c.

Maclean, John. "The Importance of Newcomers in the International Oil Business." *Middle East Economic Survey* XI, no. 24 (1968).

Manne, Alan, and Leo Schrattenholzer, International Energy Workshop. *Part I: Overview of Poll Responses* and *Part II: Frequency Responses*. Laxenburg, Austria, 1995.

Masters, C.D., D.H. Root and W.D. Dietzman. "Distribution and Quantitative Assessment of World Crude Oil Reserves and Resources." Proceedings, 11th World Petroleum Congress, 2, 1983.

— et al. "World Petroleum Assessment and Analysis." Proceedings of 14th World Petroleum Congress, Stavanger, Norway, 1994.

Matsou, Naoki and Ryuichi Higasida. "Transforming Electric Power Sector in ASEAN Countries." *Energy in Japan*. Tokyo, Japan: Institute of Energy Economics (1995).

Matsui, Kenichi. "Taiheiyou Chiiki ni Okeru Enerugi Jukyu no Sui to Kongo no Doko" (The Trend and Outlook for Energy Demand and Supply in the Pacific Region). *Enerugi Keizai* (Energy Economics). Tokyo, Japan: Institute of Energy Economics (1994).

MEEC. *LNG versus the Methanol Route for Gas Processing in the Arab World*. Beirut: Middle East Economic Consultants, 1982.

Middle East Economic Survey XI, no. 24 (1968).

Ministry of International Trade and Industry, Japan (MITI). "Action Program to Arrest Global Warming." Tokyo (1990).

Mitchell, John V. "An Oil Agenda for Europe." London: Royal Institute of International Affairs (1994).

Mohnfeld, Johan. "Implications of Structural Change." *Petroleum Economist* (July 1982).

Morita, Koji. "Will Expanding Natural Gas Use Continue? – Supply Security and Japan's Choice." *Energy in Japan*. Tokyo, Japan: Institute of Energy Economics (1993).

— "Dai Ikkai Doha Tennen Gas Kaigi" (First Doha Natural Gas Conference). *Kokusai Enerugi Doukou Bunseki* (International Energy Analysis). Tokyo, Japan: Institute of Energy Economics (1995a).

— "Steaming Coal Supply/Demand Outlook for Asia/Pacific and Japan's Subject." *Energy in Japan*. Tokyo, Japan: Institute of Energy Economics (1995b).

Mork, Knut A. "Business Cycles and the Oil Market." *Energy Journal*, Special Issue: The Changing World Petroleum Market (1994).

Nazer, Hisham. "Challenges for the Oil Producers into the 21st Century." Lecture delivered at the Second International Conference on Catalysts in Petroleum Refining and Petrochemical Industries. Kuwait, 22 April

1995, reprinted in *Middle East Economic Survey*, 1 May 1995.

Nehring, Richard. *Giant Oil Fields and World Oil Resources*. Rand Corporation R-2284-CIA, June 1978.

Niskanen, William A. "A Primer on Energy Security Policy." In *Oil and America's Security*, edited by E.R. Fried and N.M. Blandin. Washington, DC: Brookings Institution, 1988.

Ogawa, Yoshiki. "Present Situations and Problems of Overheating Chinese Oil Market." *Energy in Japan*. Tokyo, Japan: Institute of Energy Economics (1995).

OPEC. *Annual Statistical Bulletin 1993*. Vienna: OPEC, 1994.

Penrose, Edith T. "Vertical Integration with Joint Control of Raw Material Production: Crude Oil in the Middle East." *Journal of Development Studies* 1, no. 3 (April 1965).

— *The Large International Firm in Developing Countries*. London: George Allen and Unwin, 1968.

Petro Finance Market Intelligence Service. *Global Oil Markets*. Various editions.

Petroleum Finance Company and *Petroleum Intelligence Weekly, One Price for All Seasons: The Diminishing Seasonality of Oil Markets*. September 1993.

Pugliaresi, Lucian, and Anna C. Hensel. "Improvements in Progress for Russia's New PSA Law." *Oil & Gas Journal* (25 March 1996).

Reinsch, Anthony E., Jennifer I. Considine, and Edward J. Mackay. *Taxing the Difference: World Oil Market Projections 1994–2009*. Canadian Energy Research Institute, September 1994.

Riva, Jr., Joseph P. *Petroleum Exploration Opportunities in the Former Soviet Union*. Pennwell Books, 1994.

Roeber, Joe. *The Evolution of Oil Markets: Trading Instruments and Their Role in Oil Price Formation*. London: Royal Institute of International Affairs, 1993.

Samuels, Richard J. *The Business of the Japanese State: Energy Markets in Comparative and Historical Perspective*. Ithaca, NY: Cornell University Press, 1987.

Sauer, David G. "Measuring Economic Markets for Imported Crude Oil." *Energy Journal* 15, no. 2 (1994).

Seymour, Ian. *OPEC: Instrument of Change*. London: Macmillan, 1980.

Shpilman, V.I., and A.M. Brekhuntsov. "The Oil and Gas Potential of Western Siberia." Paper delivered to the Oil & Gas Workshop, US Department of Energy, Tyumen, Russia, January 1992.

Shultz, Chuck E. "Oil in the C.I.S." Twelfth International Oil and Gas Markets Conference of the Canadian Energy Research Institute, Calgary,

Alberta, 27 September 1993.

Stern, Jonathan P. *The Russian Natural Gas Bubble: Consequences for European Gas Markets*. London: Royal Institute of International Affairs, 1995.

Stevens, Paul. *Joint Ventures in Middle East Oil, 1957–1975*. Middle East Economic Consultants, 1976.

— "Saudi Arabia Oil Policy: Its Origins Implementation and Implications." In *State, Society and Economy in Saudi Arabia*, edited by T. Niblock, London: Croom Helm, 1981.

— "A Survey of Structural Change in the International Oil Industry 1945–1984." In *The Changing Structure of the World Oil Industry*, edited by D. Hawdon, London: Croom Helm, 1984a.

— "The Economics of Hydrocarbon Pipelines in the 21st Century." *Pipes and Pipelines International* (September–October 1984b).

— "Arab Downstream Petroleum Exports – Problems and Prospects." In *Middle East Exports: Problems and Prospects*. Occasional Papers Series no. 28. Durham, UK: University of Durham Centre for Middle Eastern and Islamic Studies, 1986a.

— "Oil Prices: The Start of an Era." *Energy Policy* (May 1996b).

— "OPEC and Oil Revenues." In *Trade, Transfers and Development*, edited by S. Mansoob Murshed and Kunibert Raffer, Cheltenham, UK: Edward Elgar, 1993.

— "International Developments in Energy Policy: The Context and the Theory." Presentation paper for summer seminar, Center for Petroleum and Mineral Law and Policy, University of Dundee, Dundee, 1995a.

— "The Determination of Oil Prices 1945–95: a diagrammatic interpretation." *Energy Policy* (September 1995b).

Stocking, George W. *Middle East Oil: A Study in Political and Economic Controversy*. Nashville, TN: Vanderbilt University Press, 1970.

Thomas, S.D. "Modelling UK Energy Demand to 2000." *Energy Policy* 8, no. 1 (March 1980).

Toichi, Tsutomu. "LNG Development at a Turning Point and Policy Issues for Japan." *Energy in Japan*, no. 126 (March 1994).

— and Hiroshi Kashio. "International Oil Market Outlook and Major's Asian Strategy." 300th Regular Meeting for Briefing Research Reports, Institute of Energy Economics, Tokyo, Japan, 1994.

— Kitoshi Yamazaki and Tadashi Horie. "International Oil Situation and Oil and Gas Policies of Gulf Oil-Producing Countries." Tokyo: 312th Regular Meeting for Briefing Research Reports, Institute of Energy Economics, Japan, 1995.

Totto, L., and T.M. Johnson. "OPEC Domestic Oil Demand: Product

Forecasts for 1985 and 1990." *OPEC Review*, 7 no. 2 (Summer 1993).

Tretyakova, Albina, and Meredith Heinemeier. "Cost Estimates for the Soviet Oil Industry: 1970 to 1990." Center for International Research, US Bureau of the Census, CIR Staff Paper no. 20, June 1986.

Ulmishek, Gregory F., and Charles D. Masters. "Oil, gas resources estimated in the former Soviet Union." *Oil & Gas Journal* (13 December 1993).

United Nations (ESCWA). *Arab Energy: Prospects to 2000.* McGraw-Hill, New York, 1982.

US Department of Energy. *Annual Energy Outlook.* annual.

— *International Energy Outlook.* annual.

— *International Energy Outlook 1993,* Washington, DC, 1993.

Verleger, Philip. "The Evolution of Oil as a Commodity." In *Energy: Markets and Regulation*, edited by Richard L. Gordon, Henry D. Jacoby and Martin B. Zimmerman. Cambridge, MA: MIT Press, 1987.

Watkins, Campbell. "Unravelling a Riddle: The Outlook for Russian Oil." In *The Energy Journal Special Issue: The Changing World Petroleum Market*, edited by Helmut Frank. 1994.

Weekly Petroleum Argus, 21 August 1995.

Wilson, David. *The Demand for Energy in the Soviet Union.* London: Croom Helm, 1983.

World Bank. World Tables, (1994).

— *World Development Report 1995.*

World Energy Council. *Energy for Tomorrow's World – The Realities, the Real Options and the Agenda for Achievement.* New York: St. Martin's Press, 1993.

Wu, Kang. "Oil Demand, Supply, and Refining Outlook in the Asia-Pacific Region." Presentation paper at the 8th Annual World Refining Congress held in Singapore on 12–14 June 1995, East-West Center, Hawaii, 1995.

Yamani, Zaki. "Participation Versus Nationalization: A Better Means to Survive." In *Continuity and Change in the World Oil Industry*, edited by Zahayr M. Mikdashi, Sheryl Cleland and Ian Seymour. Beirut: Middle East Research and Publishing Centre, 1970.

Yergin, Daniel. *The Prize.* New York: Simon and Schuster, 1991.

— and Thane Gustafson. *Russia 2010 and What It Means for the World.* Random House, 1993.

Zannetos, Zenon S. "Oil Tanker Markets: Continuity amidst Change." In *Energy: Markets and Regulation*, edited by Richard L. Gordon, Henry D. Jacoby and Martin B. Zimmerman, Cambridge, MA: MIT Press, 1991.

Index